World War II Administrative Histories

World War II
Administrative Histories

© Ross & Perry, Inc. 2001 All rights reserved.

No claim to U.S. government work contained throughout this book.

Protected under the Berne Convention. Published 2001

Printed in The United States of America
Ross & Perry, Inc. Publishers
717 Second St., N.E., Suite 200
Washington, D.C. 20002
Telephone (202) 675-8300
Facsimile (202) 675-8400
info@RossPerry.com

SAN 253-8555

Government Reprints Press Edition 2001

Government Reprints Press is an Imprint of Ross & Perry, Inc.

Previously printed as "Guide to United States Naval Administrative Histories of World War II" by Naval History Division.

Library of Congress Control Number: 2001093132

http://www.GPOreprints.com

ISBN 1-931641-38-2

♾ The paper used in this publication meets the requirements for permanence established by the American National Standard for Information Sciences "Permanence of Paper for Printed Library Materials" (ANSI Z39.48-1984).

All rights reserved. No copyrighted part of this publication may be reproduced, stored in a retrieval system, or transmitted, in any form or by any means, electronic, photocopying, recording, or otherwise, without the prior written permission of the publisher.

CONTENTS

	page
INTRODUCTION	v
LIST OF HISTORIES	xi

ANNOTATED GUIDE

Navy Department	1
Shore Establishment	85
Operating Forces	117

APPENDIX A

Individuals Assigned to Administrative History Project, June 1945	153
INDEX	157

INTRODUCTION

The unpublished histories described in this guide record experiences and provide insights into policies, decisions, implementing actions, and accomplishments that are of continuing value in solving the Navy's problems of today and the future. They additionally represent a valuable body of source materials for scholarly researchers in history and other fields.

Comprised of approximately 300 bound volumes, the overall collection is maintained by the Navy Department Library. The group includes narrative histories dealing with virtually every aspect of the administration of the Naval Establishment and the roles it played in assuring victory during the wide-ranging operations of World War II. Some of the volumes also contain brief coverage of the beginnings and early histories of organizations and activities.

These so-called administrative histories were one part of the Navy's effort to record its wartime experience. The first project was headed by Lieutenant Commander (later Rear Admiral) Samuel E. Morison, who early in 1942 was designated by President Franklin D. Roosevelt and Secretary of the Navy Frank Knox to prepare a history of naval operations. This led to the postwar publishing of the monumental fifteen-volume History of United States Naval Operations in World War II (Boston: Little, Brown, and Co., 1947-1962).

The second part was initiated after the President directed the establishment of a government-wide program, under the direction of the Bureau of the Budget, to document the administrative aspects of the war effort. In February 1943, Professor Robert G. Albion was charged with supervising the Navy's portion of that project, including oversight of the preparation of narrative summaries by the Offices of the Secretary of the Navy and the Chief of Naval Operations, and by the various departmental bureaus.

The Navy's historical endeavors were reorganized on 12 July 1944 when Admiral E. C. Kalbfus, USN (Ret.) was detached from the General Board and became Director of Naval History. His orders were to coordinate the various programs underway, including those of Professors Albion and Morison. Early in 1945, Admiral Kalbfus issued a series of directives relating to the writing of administrative histories. In one measure, he broadened the scope of the project beyond the Navy Department proper by requesting that major Fleet and shore-based commands submit narratives of their wartime experiences. As a result, the United States Fleet, Pacific and Atlantic Fleets, sea frontiers, naval districts, and several independent commands were added to the program.

Admiral Kalbfus's Office of Naval History also provided guidance on the desired scope of the manuscripts, recommending that emphasis be given to such topics as policy formulation, the development of administrative structure, and relationships with other commands. Commanders also were urged to encourage their historians to consult the source materials maintained by the independent Office of Naval Records and Library in Washington that was under the direction of Kalbfus's deputy, Commodore Dudley W. Knox, USN (Ret.). While some organizations utilized existing historical sections and personnel for the project, the Office of Naval History also assisted other commands in the assignment and orientation of a number of officers designated to perform historical duties.

At the end of World War II, the Office of Naval History began the writing of a single volume, based primarily on the administrative histories, that would provide a condensed analysis of the Navy Department's wartime experiences. After initial work by Professor Albion, the project was undertaken by Rear Admiral Julius A. Furer, USN (Ret.). In 1959, the Naval History Division published through the Government Printing Office Admiral Furer's volume entitled Administration of the Navy Department in World War II. As the title suggests, this comprehensive work focuses on the headquarters offices and bureaus which comprised the Navy Department. Coverage of the administration of the shore establishment and operating forces is limited to brief information of a background nature. Thus, the histories described in this guide provide an important supplement to the Furer volume.

Although the documents described herein represent the basic administrative histories of the Navy in World War II, the reader should be aware of other sources on the subject. Numerous subsidiary histories and unbound appendix materials were submitted as supplements to specific volumes in the series. That collection is held in the Operational Archives of the Naval History Division. A description of the histories included in the group appears in Partial Checklist: World War II Histories and Reports in the Naval History Division (Washington: Naval History Division, 1973). In addition, the Navy Department Library has many works bearing on the broad subject of naval administration in World War II.

Each entry in this guide lists authors when such information is contained in specific volumes. An effort to identify other contributors resulted in the location of an overall list of individuals working on the project as of June 1945. Although it by no means records the names of all writers assigned to the administrative histories, the list is reproduced as an appendix to this guide in an attempt to give credit to as many authors as possible.

According to Professor Albion, the following Naval Reserve officers served as successive principal historians for major commands and activities:

Office of Chief of Naval Operations
  Lieutenant Elting E. Morison
  Commander Duncan S. Ballantine

Bureau of Aeronautics
  Lieutenant John Jennings
  Lieutenant Commander Clifford L. Lord
  Lieutenant Commander Henry M. Dater

Bureau of Medicine and Surgery
  Lieutenant Chester L. Guthrie

Bureau of Naval Personnel
  Lieutenant Commander J. Willard Hurst

Bureau of Ordnance
  Lieutenant Bernard Brodie
  Lieutenant Commander Joseph J. Mathews

Bureau of Ships
  Lieutenant Paul J. Strayer

Bureau of Supplies and Accounts
  Lieutenant James E. Colvin

Bureau of Yards and Docks
  Commander Frank W. Herring

Commander in Chief, U. S. Fleet
  Lieutenant Commander Walter M. Whitehill

Commander in Chief, U. S. Atlantic Fleet
  Lieutenant Commander Laurance Thompson

Commander in Chief, U. S. Pacific Fleet
  Lieutenant Commander John H. Kemble

    Many individuals participated in producing this guide. Mr. Edward J. Marolda and Mr. William C. Heimdahl, of the Naval History Division's Operational Archives, are the principal compilers. They worked under the guidance of Dr. Dean C. Allard who heads the Operational Archives, and received additional advice and assistance from Mr. Walter B. Greenwood, the director of the Navy Department Library. Other members of the

Navy Department Library staff assisting in the completion of the work were Miss Mary E. Pickens and Mr. James E. Smith. The Guide's index was prepared by Mr. Marolda and Ms. Nina F. Statum. The final manuscript was typed by Mrs. R. L. Kieltyka.

The histories described in this guide can be consulted in the Navy Department Library. Microfilm or other reproduced copies of the histories also circulate under the inter-library loan system.

> EDWIN B. HOOPER
> Vice Admiral, USN (Ret.)
> Director of Naval History

LIST OF HISTORIES

NAVY DEPARTMENT

Office of the Secretary of the Navy

1. Civilian Personnel
2. Office of Procurement and Material: Industrial Mobilization
3. Office of Procurement and Material: Planning and Statistics Branch
4. Office of Procurement and Material: Production Branch
5. Office of Procurement and Material: Procurement Branch, Finance
6. Office of Procurement and Material: Coordination of Material Procurement
7. History of Navy Department Renegotiation
8. Administrative History, Office of Research and Inventions, 1 July - 31 December 1945
9. History of the Office of the Coordinator of Research and Development from 12 July 1941 to 19 May 1945

Commander in Chief, United States Fleet

10. Headquarters
11. Convoy and Routing
12. Office of the Inspector General

Office of the Chief of Naval Operations

13. Army-Navy Petroleum Board and Petroleum and Tanker Division
14. Internal Security and Passive Defense
15. Mine Warfare in the Naval Establishment
16. Naval Communications
17. The Control of Naval Logistics

18. Aspects of Logistics Planning
19. The Evolution of the Lend-Lease Office of Record
20. The Logistics of Fleet Readiness: The Fleet Maintenance Division in World War II
21. The Logistics of Advance Bases
22. Procurement Organization under the Chief of Naval Operations: The History of OP-24
23. Military Government
24. Shipping in Naval Logistics
25. Technical Mission in Europe
26. Office of Naval Intelligence

<u>Office of the Deputy Chief of Naval Operations (Air)</u>

27. Aviation in the Office of the Chief of Naval Operations
28. History of Naval Aviation
29. The Navy's Air War: Mission Completed
30. Financial and Legislative Planning, 1911-1945
31. Aviation Planning
32. Aviation Shore Establishments, 1911-1945
33. Aviation Training, 1911-1939
34. Aviation Training, 1940-1945
35. The Civil Aeronautics Administration-War Training Service (Navy) Flight Training Program
36. Aviation in the Fleet Exercises, 1911-1939
37. Procurement of Naval Aircraft, 1907-1939
38. Aviation Procurement, 1939-1945
39. The Navy's Transport Glider Program, 1941-1943
40. Aviation Personnel, 1911-1939
41. Aviation Personnel, 1939-1945
42. Air Task Organization in the Pacific Ocean Areas: Task Organization of Ship-Based Aircraft
43. Air Task Organization in Pacific Ocean Areas: Task Organization of Land-Based Aircraft

    44. The Development of Fleet Air Wings
    45. Air Task Organization in the Atlantic Ocean Area

Office of the Commandant, United States Marine Corps

    46. United States Marine Corps

Bureau of Aeronautics

    47. Summary
    48. Background
    49. Organization and Administration
    50. Operational Responsibilities
    51. Determination of Military Characteristics
    52. Aviation Planning
    53. Procurement, Production and Contracts
    54. Naval Aviation Inspection
    55. Maintenance
    56. Material and Supply
    57. Research, Technical Developments, and Engineering
    58. Aviation Shore Establishments
    59. Aviation Personnel and Training
    60. Budget Planning and Administration
    61. Naval Aviation Photography and Motion Pictures
    62. Aerology
    63. Publications
    64. Foreign Aid
    65. Aviation Medicine
    66. Air Intelligence
    67. Marine Corps Aviation

Bureau of Medicine and Surgery

    68. United States Navy Medical Department at War, 1941-1945 (operations)
    69. United States Navy Medical Department at War, 1941-1945 (administration)

Bureau of Ordnance

70. Organization, Administration, and Special Functions
71. Planning
72. Procurement
73. Research and Development, Maintenance
74. Personnel and Training, Finance, Special Board, Legal Counsel
75. Guns and Mounts
76. Armor, Projectiles, Ammunition Details, Bombs and Plastics
77. Rockets, Explosives and Propellants, Pyrotechnics
78. Underwater Ordnance
79. Fire Control (Except Radar) and Aviation Ordnance

Bureau of Naval Personnel

80. Preface: Structure of the Bureau
81. Planning and Control Activity
82. Officer Personnel
83. Training Activity
84. The Negro in the Navy in World War II
85. The Welfare Activity
86. Chaplains' Division; Records and Transportation Activity; Office of Public Information; Administrative Services
87. History of the Enlisted Personnel Activity
88. History of the Women's Reserve

Bureau of Ships

89. An Administrative History of the Bureau of Ships During World War II

Bureau of Supplies and Accounts

90. Accounting Group and Disbursing Division
91. Supplying the Aeronautical Establishment
92. History of the Clothing Division

93. Wartime History of the Cost Inspection Service
94. History of the Fuel Division
95. History of the Stock Division
96. History of the Maintenance Division
97. History -- International Aid Division
98. Packaging and Materials Handling
99. History of Officer Personnel Division; History of Chief Clerk's Division
100. Supplying the Fleet
101. Administrative Planning Division; History of Advanced Base Section and the Logistic Planning Division (December 1942 - April 1945) - Supplying the Advanced Bases
102. First Draft of Administrative History of Supply Corps Procurement in World War II (Interim Report)
103. A History of Purchasing within the Supply Group, World War II
104. Historical Record of the Subsistence Division
105. Synopsis of Ship's Store Division Accomplishments, 1 June 1944 to 1 September 1945
106. History of the Storage Division
107. History of the Transportation Division

Bureau of Yards and Docks

108. Building the Navy's Bases in World War II; History of the Bureau of Yards and Docks and the Civil Engineer Corps, 1940-1946

SHORE ESTABLISHMENT

Naval Districts

109. History of Naval Administration, World War II (First Naval District)
110. Historical Summary of the Third Naval District

111. The War History of the Fourth Naval District from Dec 7th 1941
112. History of the Fifth Naval District, 1939-1945
113. History of the Sixth Naval District
114. Administrative History of the Seventh Naval District, 1 February 1942 - 14 August 1945
115. History of the Eighth Naval District
116. Administrative History (Ninth Naval District)
117. Administrative Narrative (Tenth Naval District)
118. Administrative History (Eleventh Naval District)
119. Administrative History, Twelfth Naval District, 1939-1945
120. Administrative History of the Thirteenth Naval District
121. Administrative History of the Fourteenth Naval District and the Hawaiian Sea Frontier
122. Administrative History, 15th Naval District and Panama Sea Frontier

Chief of Naval Operations Activities

123. Hydrographic Office
124. U. S. Naval Observatory
125. School of Oriental Languages
126. Naval Air Test Center, Patuxent River, Maryland

Bureau of Ordnance Activities

127. Selected Ammunition Depots
128. Ordnance Plants
129. U. S. Naval Gun Factory
130. Naval Torpedo Station, Newport, Rhode Island
131. The History of the Naval Ordnance Laboratory, 1918-1945
132. Miscellaneous Activities

Bureau of Supplies and Accounts Activities

133. U. S. Naval Supply Depot, Oakland, California as of 31 December 1944

Other Shore Activities*

    134. War History of the Naval Research Laboratory
    135. Narrative History of the Potomac River Naval Command
    136. Administrative History of Severn River Naval Command
    137. The United States Naval Academy and World War II

OPERATING FORCES

Atlantic

    138. Commander in Chief, U. S. Atlantic Fleet
    139. Commander Task Force Twenty-Four
    140. Commander Greenland Patrol
    141. An Administrative History of Destroyers, Atlantic Fleet
    142. Air Force Atlantic Fleet History
    143. Commander Fleet Operational Training Command
    144. Administrative History of Commander Service Force, U. S. Atlantic Fleet, during World War II
    145. A History of the Amphibious Training Command, United States Atlantic Fleet and its Antecedent the Amphibious Force, United States Atlantic Fleet
    146. Commander South Atlantic Force
    147. Administrative History, United States Naval Forces in Europe 1940-1946
    148. Naval Forces, Northwest African Waters and the Eighth Fleet

---

*Note: Additional histories of some shore establishments are contained in the histories of parent headquarters commands.

Pacific

149. Commander in Chief, United States Pacific Fleet and Pacific Ocean Areas, Command History
150. History of the Amphibious Forces, U. S. Pacific Fleet
151. Administrative Study of Commander Destroyers/Cruisers Pacific Fleet during World War II
152. History of the Fleet Operational Training Command, Pacific
153. Administrative History of Minecraft Pacific Fleet
154. Motor Torpedo Boat Squadrons
155. History of Service Force
156. Administrative History of the North Pacific Area
157. Administrative History of the ComMarGils Area
158. Administrative History of the Forward Area, Central Pacific and the Marianas Area
159. Commander U. S. Naval Forces, Southwest Pacific

Sea Frontiers and Operating Bases

160. Administrative History of the Caribbean Sea Frontier to VE-Day
161. History of the Eastern Sea Frontier (Organizational and Operational)
162. History of the Gulf Sea Frontier, 6 February 1942 - 14 August 1945
163. Administrative History of Western Sea Frontier during World War II
164. Aruba-Curacao Command Headquarters, Commander All Forces (Caribbean Sea Frontier)
165. The Guantanamo Sector, Caribbean Sea Frontier and the U. S. Naval Operating Base, Guantanamo Bay, Cuba

166. An Administrative History of the U. S. Naval Operating Base Trinidad, B. W. I. and the Trinidad Sector of the Caribbean Sea Frontier, 7 December 1941 to August 1945
167. Commandant N. O. B. Bermuda
168. Naval Operating Base, Iceland
169. Administrative History of the Naval Operating Base, Terminal Island (San Pedro), California

Topical Histories

170. Submarine Commands
171. An Administrative History of PT's in World War II
172. Arming of Merchant Ships and Naval Armed Guard Service
173. History of the Naval Armed Guard Afloat, World War II

NAVY DEPARTMENT

Office of the Secretary of the Navy

1. Executive Office of the Secretary of the Navy, "Civilian Personnel." 3 vols. Washington, n.d. 1,630 pp., appendices.

    The two narrative volumes of this history discuss the Navy's employment of civilian manpower from 1940 to 1945. Several aspects of the program are examined, including its organization and extent. Efforts to resolve the numerous problems involved in the procurement, training, and assignment of the large number of new employees resulting from rapid wartime expansion, also are treated at length. Major emphasis is devoted to utilization of civilians at shore establishments in the United States, although one chapter considers the placement of these workers at offshore bases. The extensive volume of appendices contains such source materials as organizational charts, letters, memoranda, and reports.

    Most of this history was written by Captain Samuel H. Ordway, Jr., USNR, who also performed the duties of overall editor. Other sections were drafted by Lieutenants James C. George, USNR, and Daniel R. Howe, USNR; Commanders Frank Cushman, USNR, and H. Lee White, USNR; and Captain John Craig, USNR.

2.	Executive Office of the Secretary of the Navy, "Office of Procurement and Material: Industrial Mobilization." Washington. n.d.

This volume is a series of thirty-eight memoranda and accompanying documents that provide brief summaries of various aspects of the Navy's role in the wartime mobilization of industrial production. The first few memoranda concern the relationship of the Navy to the functions of the War Production Board. The remaining memoranda discuss the Navy's involvement in obtaining essential raw materials, including carbon, copper, and rubber, as well as the procurement of a myriad of finished products. Attached charts, graphs, and orders furnish supplementary data.

3.	Executive Office of the Secretary of the Navy, "Office of Procurement and Material: Planning and Statistics Branch." 4 vols. Washington. 1945. Appendices.

Following an explanation of its origins and organization, the branch's activities from establishment in early 1942 until dissolution in February 1945 are detailed. Among those activities were the development of centralized and uniform accounting systems; the establishment of controls over procurement schedules, raw materials, and inventories; and the analysis of the status and progress of such programs. A lengthy discussion is devoted to the branch's assistance to the Navy Department's bureaus, the Marine Corps, and the Coast Guard in developing similar programs. Its role as the central issuing authority for statistical information to the War Production Board and other agencies also is examined.

Three appendices are mentioned in the table of contents of the narrative volume. However, only Appendix B is included. It appears in three volumes and comprises important memoranda, letters, directives, and reports on procurement and material programs.

4. Executive Office of the Secretary of the Navy, "Office of Procurement and Material: Production Branch." Washington. 1945. 199 pp.

Derived from an earlier analysis of the Production Branch's wartime activities, this study covers the period from 31 January 1942 to 31 January 1945. A case history approach is used to discuss the branch's varied duties, including its effort to coordinate and insure production of materials essential to the Navy's operation and the allocation of those materials in order to avoid deficiencies and promote conservation.

Each case history examines specific raw materials such as steel, copper, and aluminum, or finished products such as electronics equipment. Introductory sections describe the organization of the branch, its personnel, and personnel procedures. The branch's liaison activity with the War Production Board is an important topic considered throughout the volume. The analysis that served as a basis for this history was prepared by a group of naval officers under the coordination of Lieutenant Commander L. Rohe Walker, USNR.

5. Executive Office of the Secretary of the Navy "Office of Procurement and Material: Procurement Branch, Finance." Washington. 1946. 35 pp., appendices.

An introductory narrative provides a brief history of the Finance Division of the Procurement Branch during the period from May 1942 to August 1945. The history concentrates on the division's program of extending government credit through war production loans authorized by Executive Order No. 9112. The development of the numerous policies and procedures involved in the loan program also is discussed. A roster of Finance Division personnel follows the narrative.

At the beginning of the extensive appendices, the location of the documentary material referred to in the footnotes to the narrative is outlined in a short bibliography. Much of this source material, as well as numerous other policy statements, directives, memoranda, and reports, is included in the remaining appendices.

The author of the narrative was Lieutenant Commander Theodore Chase, USNR.

6.   Executive Office of the Secretary of the Navy, "Office of Procurement and Material: Coordination of Material Procurement." 11 vols. Washington. n.d.

These volumes contain compilations of source materials related to the diverse functions of the Office of Procurement and Material. Memoranda, orders, charts, photographs, and published items pertaining to such activities as procurement, production, inventory control, and inspection administration are among the numerous documents included. Narrative sections are not included in the volumes.

7.   Office of the Under Secretary of the Navy, "History of Navy Department Renegotiation." 5 vols. Washington. 1947. Appendices.

Volume I of this series is divided into three parts. The first provides a brief historical summary of American efforts to control excessive profits on war contracts. Also discussed are the provisions of renegotiation legislation and criticism of this legislation by opponents. The organization, procedures, and personnel of the Navy Price Adjustment Board, the office responsible for renegotiation activity, is the subject of Part II. Part III sets forth various observations concerning statutory, organizational, and operational aspects of renegotiation, and contains suggestions for similar efforts in the future.

The Price Adjustment Board's method of processing cases is reviewed in Volume II. Also included is a detailed examination of the organization and functions of the divisions of the board. This treatment, as well as a section on the personnel of the board, provides more thorough coverage of subjects found in Part II of the first volume. Volume III contains extensive statistics relating to the board's activities. Among this material are eighty-six tables and seven charts.

Two volumes of appendices, one each for Volumes I and II, accompany the set. Numerous administrative, procedural, and legal memoranda referred to in the narrative are included in the appendices, along with copies of several manuals on such subjects as the renegotiation of construction contracts. The author of the history was Robert J. H. Powel, Special Assistant to the Under Secretary of the Navy.

8. Executive Office of The Secretary of the Navy, "Administrative History, Office of Research and Inventions, 1 July - 31 December 1945." Washington. 1948. 196 pp., appendices.

This volume opens with a brief summary of the establishment of the Office of Research and Inventions in May 1945. The new office included the Naval Research Laboratory, the Office of

Patents and Inventions, the Office of the Coordinator of Research and Development, and the Special Devices Division of the Bureau of Aeronautics. Following an outline of the office's basic policies and structure, the remainder of the narrative examines the activities and historical origins of all the divisions except that of the Research Laboratory.

The narrative is followed by a series of nineteen appendices that include copies of key directives, short biographies of important personnel, pertinent general orders, and selected reports. A copy of Rear Admiral Julius A. Furer's administrative history of the Office of the Coordinator of Research and Development and a catalogue of training devices also are located in the appendices. The authors of the volume were Lieutenants (junior grade) Donald Jackson, USNR, and Louise Herring.

9. Executive Office of the Secretary of the Navy, "History of the Office of the Coordinator of Research and Development from 12 July 1941 to 19 May 1945." Washington. 1945. 28 pp., appendices.

This history discusses the origin and development of scientific research in the Navy, the establishment of the Office of the Coordinator of Research and Development in 1941, its relationship to other offices and agencies, and the office's internal organization. Particular attention is given to an explanation of the policies and procedures that were developed by the office during World War II.

Appendices include organizational flow charts, biographical sketches of key personnel, and descriptions of major projects undertaken by the office. The author, Rear Admiral Julius A. Furer, USN, served as Coordinator of Research and Development from 13 December 1941 to 19 May 1945.

An October 1961 addendum prepared by him has been added at the beginning of the narrative.

Commander in Chief, United States Fleet

10. Commander in Chief, United States Fleet, "Headquarters," Washington. 1946. 178 pp., appendices.

This history dicusses the organization and administration of Headquarters, Commander in Chief, United States Fleet (COMINCH). The narrative begins with a chapter tracing the evolution of COMINCH from December 1941 to its disestablishment in October 1945. The ensuing chapters deal with the functions of the divisions responsible for plans, operations, readiness, and combat intelligence. The two final chapters briefly describe the activities of the Tenth Fleet and the Office of the Naval Inspector General.

In addition to the considerable number of documents reprinted in the narrative section, the nineteen appendices contain copies of important executive orders, letters, and memoranda outlining the functions and organization of COMINCH headquarters. Three organizational charts and several rosters of officers, issued periodically throughout the war, also are included in this section. The author of the history was Commander Walter Muir Whitehill, USNR.

11.   Commander in Chief, United States Fleet, "Convoy and Routing." Washington. 1945. 147 pp., appendices.

The administration of the Convoy and Routing Section of the Tenth Fleet is the subject of this volume. The section's administrative evolution and its mission of insuring the safe movement of merchant ships and troop transports are outlined in Chapter One. A lengthy discussion of the aid given to ships sailing independently and to ships in convoys follows. The narrative details the procedures and policies devised to protect merchantmen from enemy submarine attack. Procedures for avoiding and minimizing other navigational dangers also are related. The discussion of convoys focuses primarily on the North Atlantic, although a few remarks pertain to similar activity in the Pacific. A short concluding chapter summarizes the overall effort of the Convoy and Routing Section.

Eighty pages of appendices contain numerous tables, graphs, and photographs. Also included are lists of abbreviations, sources, and officers of the section. The only author identified is Commander George P. Markoff, USNR, who prepared the chapter dealing with communications systems used to report ship movements.

12.   Commander in Chief, United States Fleet, "Office of the Inspector General." Washington, 1945. 15 pp., appendices.

The greater part of this manuscript consists of documentary material. In a short introductory narrative there is a description of the establishment of the Office of the Inspector General in May 1942 and its duties of inquiring into and reporting upon any matter affecting the efficiency and economy of the naval service. Besides comparing the office to that of the Inspector General of the Army, the narrative also surveys the evolution of inspection activities throughout the history of the Navy Department. The latter subject is developed more fully in a lengthy history located among the appendices that details such efforts from the formal establishment of the Navy Department in 1798 to the eve of World War II.

The other appendices contain considerable documentation regarding recommendations for the establishment of an Inspector General, advice received from the Army Inspector General, and tentative guidelines for inspection procedures. Key directives which established the office, and a lengthy 1944 memorandum that includes a summary of all naval inspection activities at the time, comprise the remaining appendices.

Office of the Chief of Naval Operations

13.   Office of the Chief of Naval Operations, "Army-Navy Petroleum Board and Petroleum and Tanker Division (CNO)." 4 vols. Washington. n.d. 299 pp., appendices.

The narrative volume of this set is divided into three parts. Part I deals with the Army-Navy Petroleum Board; Part II treats the Petroleum and Tanker Division of the Office of the Chief of Naval Operations; and a very brief third part discusses the Allied Tanker Coordinating Committees.

The efforts of the Petroleum Board to coordinate the procurement, storage, and shipping of petroleum products by the Navy and the Army are examined in Part I. After outlining the organization of the board and the functions of area petroleum officers, the narrative continues with a series of chapters explaining the particular activities of the working sections of the board.

A final chapter evaluates the board's policy-making function.

The approach used in Part II differs slightly from that of Part I. Although both the organization and functions of the Petroleum and Tanker Division are discussed, the major emphasis is on the problems dealt with during World War II. Among these was the task of maximizing the efficient operation of the ships used to transport petroleum.

The final part of the narrative briefly describes the composition and purpose of two Allied Tanker Coordinating Committees located in Washington and London. Also noted are the general policies developed by the committee. A glossary of abbreviations and a subject index follow the narrative.

The appendices to the history are divided into three volumes. The first contains a group of sixty-two general documents. Among these are directives, letters and memoranda, as well as statistical tables, rosters of officers, and minutes of selected meetings. Of particular value is a ten-page capsule history of the functions and operations of the Army-Navy Petroleum Board. Volume II of the appendices is a lengthy analysis by L. W. Harford of the British Ministry of Fuel and Power entitled "A Review of Petroleum Supply - North African Theater 1942-1943." Copies of monthly reports of the Army-Navy Petroleum Board from December 1944 to July 1945 are included in the third volume of appendices.

The author of most of the narrative and the overall editor was Captain Alfred F. Loomis, USNR, who was assisted by Lieutenant Bernard McKenna, USNR. Additional chapters were written by Lieutenant V. P. Selph, (SC) USNR, and Lieutenant Colonel D. M. S. Langworthy of the British Army.

14.   Office of the Chief of Naval Operations, "Internal Security and Passive Defense." Washington. n.d. 56 pp.

   This history discusses the work of the Internal Security Section of the Base Maintenance Division. The section was responsible for safeguarding private facilities, particularly shipyards, with which the Navy contracted for ship construction and other work. These duties required the development of security policies and procedures, and coordination with other naval and non-naval organizations interested in the protection of private maritime installations. Such agencies included the Federal Bureau of Investigation, the Maritime Commission, and Army Provost Marshal, the Office of Naval Intelligence, and the Bureau of Yards and Docks. Three case histories are presented in this narrative to illustrate the actual functioning of the Internal Security Section.

15.   Office of the Chief of Naval Operations, "Mine Warfare in the Naval Establishment." Washington. n.d. 230 pp.

   After a brief discussion of the Navy's development of mine warfare from 1918 to 1938, this volume concentrates on the history of the Mine Warfare Section of the Base Maintenance Division during World War II. The major responsibilities of the section were research and development of mine warfare weapons, coordinating the production of such devices, and general supervision of mine warfare personnel. In addition, the section was concerned with the preparation of operational plans, the development of mine warfare countermeasures, and the collection and dissemination of information pertaining to both weapons and countermeasures.

   The narrative is divided into three basic parts. The first consists of an introductory chapter discussing the status of mine warfare in the Navy from 1918 to 1938, while the second focuses on developments in mine warfare organization and administration during the war years. The final part deals with operational activities of the section during the war.

16. Office of the Chief of Naval Operations, "Naval Communications." Washington. 1948. 370 pp., appendix.

After tracing briefly the evolution of naval communications from the creation of the Naval Radio Service in 1912, this volume focuses on the administrative history of the Division of Naval Communications from 1939 to the end of World War II. During this period, the division, which had cognizance over radio, telegraph, and telephone communications, experienced considerable expansion and underwent various organizational changes.

The operation of several offices within the division receive detailed examination. Among these are the shore section, with responsibilities for communications originating on shore; the fleet section; and the aeronautical section, which handled aircraft and air base communications and facilities. Also treated is the registered publications section that maintained and distributed certain secret and confidential publications in addition to operating a mail and courier service.

The appendix consists of a history of the Naval Teletypewriter System (NTX) during the war. The volume also includes several charts and plates as well as an index.

17. Office of the Chief of Naval Operations, "The Control of Naval Logistics." Washington. n.d. 170 pp., appendix.

During World War II, the Office of the Assistant Chief of Naval Operations (Material) underwent various changes in title, organization, and responsibility. Despite these changes, all of which are outlined in the history, the office had continuing responsibility for the execution of material plans. In performing this logistics function, the office had authority over several components of the Office of the Chief of Naval Operations, including Fleet Maintenance, Electronics, Naval Transportation, and the Progress Sections.

Most of this narrative concentrates on the administration and activities of the Progress Section, which was created in November 1942 to aid in the processing, scheduling, and coordinating of logistics plans and to monitor the execution of the plans. The final chapter evaluates several general problems confronted during the war years and offers recommendations for the management of the office in future crises.

A lengthy appendix includes copies of key directives, memoranda, and periodic statements of mission. Several lists of projects monitored by the Progress Section and assignment of its personnel also are located in this section.

18. Office of the Chief of Naval Operations, "Aspects of Logistics Planning." Washington. n.d. 206 pp.

The Logistics Plans Division was a central agency concerned with planning and organizing naval logistics support in World War II. After a lengthy introduction tracing the history of planning within the Navy from the time of

Alfred Thayer Mahan, this narrative outlines the administrative structure and duties of the office after its establishment in December 1942. The ensuing discussion details the division's activities during 1943 and early 1944, an especially busy period. In April 1944, some of its duties were assumed by the Logistics Planning Unit of the Office of the Chief of Naval Operations. A final chapter evaluates the overall accomplishments of the office.

The bibliography in Duncan S. Ballantine's <u>U. S. Naval Logistics in the Second World War</u> identifies the authors of this history as Lieutenant Myron P. Gilmore, USNR, and Lieutenant J. Blum, USNR.

19. Office the Chief of Naval Operations, "The Evolution of the Lend-Lease Office of Record." Washington. n.d. 53 pp.

According to the introduction, this volume describes "the Navy's interest...in allocation to foreign governments of naval munitions." The discussion begins by noting origins of this office in the period prior to the Lend-Lease Act, when the Navy participated in negotiations concerning foreign contracts for naval material. Part II of the narrative examines the period during which the office became the Navy's major procurement agency for the naval equipment provided foreign governments under lend-lease agreements. After the nation's entry into war, the office's role increased as it became responsible not only for procurement but also for the final assignment of naval munitions to the various Allies. This latter subject is reviewed in the final section of the history.

20.   Office of the Chief of Naval Operations, "The Logistics of Fleet Readiness: The Fleet Maintenance Division in World War II." Washington. n.d. 178 pp., appendices.

During World War II, the Fleet Maintenance Division was responsible for coordinating construction, repair, and disposal of the Navy's vessels. To achieve coordination, the division worked closely with other divisions within the Office of the Chief of Naval Operations, the material bureaus in the Navy Department, and other entities engaged in naval logistics.

Before examining the division's wartime responsibilities, the history traces the evolution of the fleet maintenance function from the creation of the Office of the Chief of Naval Operations in 1915. The narrative that follows deals with such activities as the division's shipbuilding and alteration program. A separate chapter focuses on the process involved in scheduling the availability of naval ships so that the Navy was assured of the greatest possible strength afloat. Other chapters consider the division's efforts to maintain submarines and amphibious vessels. Administration of ship decommissioning and disposal is discussed in the final chapter.

The two appendices consist of organizational charts representing the various sections of the division and depicting their duties.

Duncan S. Ballantine notes in U. S. Naval Logistics in the Second World War that the author of the history was Lieutenant (junior grade) William C. Askew, USNR.

21.   Office of the Chief of Naval Operations, "The Logistics of Advance Bases." Washington. n.d. 196 pp., appendices.

This history describes the efforts of the Base Maintenance Division in planning and coordinating logistics support for the establishment of new overseas naval bases. Beginning with an evaluation of the prewar need for more naval facilities, the narrative covers the period from 1936 through the end of the war. Activities related to base construction in the Pacific receive considerable attention, although one chapter, "Internal Organization of Op-30," presents a thorough discussion of the administrative structure of the division.

Appendices include copies of several shipment schedules, representative memoranda, and several charts. According to Duncan S. Ballantine's U. S. Naval Logistics in the Second World War, the author of this volume was Lieutenant John H. Gleason, USNR.

22. Office of the Chief of Naval Operations, "Procurement Organization under the Chief of Naval Operations: The History of Op-24." Washington. n.d. 58 pp., appendix, index.

The Materials Division existed as a distinct organization within the Office of the Chief of Naval Operations for less than three months from 27 October 1941 to 30 January 1942. Its responsibility was to work with other government agencies in planning industrial mobilization, and to coordinate the procurement, stockpiling, conservation, and allocation of materials essential to the Navy. In addition to reviewing the reasons for the division's establishment and its activities, this volume briefly analyzes attempts by the military, dating from the World War I period, to plan procurement and allocation of raw materials. The latter discussion includes a brief history of the Army and Navy Munitions Board during the interwar years.

Key documents referred to in the text are found in the appendix. The volume contains a helpful index.

23. Office of the Chief of Naval Operations, "Military Government." 3 vols. Washington. 1946. 242 pp., appendices.

The first volume of this set is divided into two parts and focuses on administrative aspects of the Navy's participation in the military government of areas liberated or occupied by the Allies during World War II. Part I of the narrative concentrates on the establishment and functioning of the Occupied Areas Section of the Office of the Chief of Naval Operations. This section was responsible for the administration of occupied areas assigned to the Navy and the training of officer personnel who staffed the area governments. Much of its effort involved planning as well as coordination with other naval activities, including the various Navy Department bureaus and the Office of Naval Intelligence.

The initial discussion is supplemented with a commentary on training and other features of military government and by a lengthy memorandum concerning the history of naval military government prepared by Captain H. L. Pence, USN, who was in charge of the Occupied Areas Section. The concluding chapter of the first part outlines the organization and responsibilities of the Office of Island Governments from April 1944 to December 1945. This office eventually assumed the duties of the Occupied Areas Section. Certain appendix documents, including copies of important memoranda, organizational charts, and published articles are included in the narrative.

The second part of the first volume contains histories of the two principal institutions used for training officers assigned to

military government duties. One of these
schools was operated at Columbia University,
while the other was at Princeton University.
Such topics as the administration, staffing,
and curriculum of the school are considered in
each history. Among the appendices to these
histories are copies of directives, reports,
and course descriptions.

The second and third volumes of the set
contain appendix material. Weekly summaries of
the activities of the Occupied Areas Office
from 26 July 1943 to 15 July 1944 are collected
in Volume II. The third volume is a compilation of miscellaneous documents related to military government.

24.   Office of the Chief of Naval Operations,
"Shipping in Naval Logistics." Washington.
n.d. 351 pp.

The Naval Transportation Service existed
in the Office of the Chief of Naval Operations
with slightly varying names since World War I.
During World War II, its functions included the
determination of shipping requirements for the
Navy and the procurement of merchant-type
vessels from the War Shipping Administration.
It also planned the transportation of personnel
and supplies and coordinated a tanker service
to meet naval fuel requirements.

Following a chronological format, six narrative chapters review the organization and
administration of the Naval Transportation Service in carrying out its functions, from the
prewar period to the end of hostilities with
Japan. The problems encountered by the service,
and its relations with the War Shipping Administration, also are discussed. The work is fully
documented. The final chapter of the volume
provides an overall assessment of the wartime
experience of the service.

25.   Office of the Chief of Naval Operations, "Technical Mission in Europe." Washington. 1945. 279 pp., appendix.

Established on 26 December 1944, the Naval Technical Mission in Europe was assigned the duty of collecting German scientific and technical information for use by the Navy's technical bureaus and the Coordinator of Research Development. The mission was activated on 20 January 1945 and was decommissioned, upon completion of its assignment, on 1 November 1945. During the nine months of its existence, a massive amount of information was compiled and transmitted to Washington in approximately 240 letter reports and 350 technical reports.

After providing a brief summary of the mission, the narrative focuses on its internal organization while in Europe. This discussion is followed by an examination of the mission's relations with various commands, including U. S. and British naval activities and the Supreme Headquarters, Allied Expeditionary Force. The methods and procedures used in preparing reports, in handling captured enemy documents and equipment, and in dealing with captured German personnel are treated. A summary reviewing the deficiencies and strengths of the mission concludes the narrative.

In addition to the extensive appendix, the volume contains rosters of both naval and civilian personnel associated with the mission and a list of the reports that they prepared. The appendix provides copies of important letters and memoranda. Several graphs showing the progress of the mission also are included.

26.   Office of the Chief of Naval Operations, "Office of Naval Intelligence." 4 vols. Washington. n.d. 1,510 pp., appendices.

Created in 1882, the Office of Naval Intelligence (ONI) had numerous responsibilities throughout its existence. Among the most important was the collection, analysis, and dissemination of information concerning the naval policies and activities of all countries.

ONI's history through 1945 is traced in three textual volumes. The narrative begins by discussing creation of the office and its general evolution to 1939. A more lengthy description of its organizational development and expanded activities during 1939-1945 follows. The remaining fourteen chapters detail the evolution, duties, and administration of each of the office's branches. Among the branches treated is the Office of Naval Records and Library, a predecessor of the Naval History Division.

A supplementary volume contains extensive appendices. Among these are copies of important memoranda, several reports, and a number of organizational charts. A few lists of publications and rosters of personnel are included.

Office of the Deputy Chief of Naval Operations (Air)

27. Office of the Deputy Chief of Naval Operations (Air), "Aviation in the Office of the Chief of Naval Operations." Washington. n.d. 134 pp.

The establishment in 1943 of the Office of the Deputy Chief of Naval Operations (Air) and its wartime evolution are examined in this brief history. The narrative also traces prewar and early wartime aviation programs. The history focuses on the development of naval aviation policy. Among specific topics treated are the views of naval bureaus regarding aviation organization and the influence of public opinion on the reorganization of naval aviation. The impact of a study, undertaken by Admiral H. E. Yarnell, USN, to determine the attitudes of naval officers regarding naval airpower also is analyzed.

28. Office of the Deputy Chief of Naval Operations (Air), "History of Naval Aviation." Vol. III: "1898-1917," Vol. IV: "1917-1918," Vol. V: "1918-1926," Vol. VI: "1926-1939." Washington. 1946. 1,438 pp.

Divided into four volumes, this history traces the evolution of naval aviation from the days of early experimentation to the eve of America's entry into World War II. The first volume focuses on the period before World War I, while the second examines the organization and administration of aviation activities and facilites during the war. The interwar years are treated in the last two volumes, with detailed discussions devoted to such topics as the creation of the Bureau of Aeronautics, the General Billy Mitchell controversy, the Morrow Board, Army-Navy relations regarding aviation, and preparedness efforts prior to World War II.

These volumes are well-documented with numerous footnotes. A helpful bibliographical essay appears at the end of the fourth volume. The author of the history was Lieutenant Commander Clifford L. Lord, USNR. A shorter version of this work, written by Lord and Archibald D. Turnbull, was published by the Yale University Press in 1949 under the title History of United States Naval Aviation.

29.   Office of the Deputy Chief of Naval Operations (Air), "The Navy's Air War: Mission Completed." Vol. VII. Washington. 1946. 594 pp., appendices.

Coverage of both the combat and administrative aspects of naval air power during the war years is presented in this concise history. The volume initially considers the development of naval aviation during the first three decades of the twentieth century and the organization of the air arm in World War II. The narrative then turns to a review of air operations in the Atlantic and Pacific theaters.

The remaining chapters are devoted to logistical matters. Such topics as training, aircraft production, expansion of the shore establishment, the role of the Naval Air Transportation Service, and scientific contributions to aviation are discussed in turn.

Two appendices provide a list of aircraft designations and a chronology of important events. The volume was edited by Lieutenant A. R. Buchanan, USNR. This work subsequently was published in 1946 by Harper and Brothers.

30.   Office of the Deputy Chief of Naval Operations (Air), "Financial and Legislative Planning, 1911-1945." Vols. VIII-IX. Washington. 1946. 547 pp.

Divided into two volumes, one for 1911 to 1933 and the other for 1934 to 1945, this work summarizes the history of financial and legislative planning activities pertaining to naval aviation. Organized chronologically with a section for each fiscal year, the discussion covers both preparation of financial estimates for submission to Congress and the administration of funds appropriated annually by that body. The analysis is based primarily on the points brought out in official testimony before the House Naval Affairs Committee and Appropriations Committee and in various Senate hearings. Plans that were implemented as a result of congressional funding, as well as those that were curtailed or postponed due to the level of appropriations, are examined.

The text includes excerpts from many key documents and is footnoted. Several charts also are located in the text. Lieutenant Charles F. Stanwood, USNR, was the author of the work.

31. Office of the Deputy Chief of Naval Operations (Air), "Aviation Planning." Vol. X Washington. n.d. 252 pp., appendices.

For the most part, the focus of this volume is on the duties and work of the Program Planning Section and the Programs and Allocations Section of the Aviation Planning Division. The primary responsibility of these sections was the planning of aviation procurement and aviation manpower programs.

Instead of adhering to a strictly chronological sequence, this narrative follows a topical organization. Among the topics presented is an explanation of the planning process itself, which is defined as "the methods and techniques...devised by staff planners to keep their analyses systematic and realistic, rather than random and based on guesswork...." About two-thirds of the volume is composed of a series of twenty-five exhibits, including memoranda, reports, and instructions.

32.	Office of the Deputy Chief of Naval Operations (Air), "Aviation Shore Establishments, 1911-1945." Vol. XI. Washington. n.d. 497 pp., appendices.

    The first of the two parts in this volume provides an extensive history of the naval aviation shore establishment between 1911 and 1938. In addition to examining the development of base complexes, the narrative notes the operational and logistical considerations that were instrumental in the establishment of each station. The effect of the submarine and the influence of America's allies on the establishment of North American and European bases during World War I are analysed. The expansion of aviation facilities during that conflict, as well as the rapid postwar reduction of operational bases, is traced. Details are included on costs of construction, maintenance, and operation of the bases. The history also covers Marine Corps air facilities. An excellent bibliography follows the narrative.

    The period from 1938 to 1945 is considered in a more limited manner in the second part of the volume. Among the topics dealt with are the building of new air stations and the expansion of existing air facilities. The development of the Naval Air Station at Quonset Point, Rhode Island is explored as a case study. The appendix to this part contains copies of a number of basic planning documents.

    Lieutenant Ivor D. Spencer, USNR, was the author of the first part, and Lieutenant Donald M. Forester, USNR, prepared the second section.

33.	Office of the Deputy Chief of Naval Operations (Air), "Aviation Training, 1911-1939." Vol. XIII. Washington. n.d. 321 pp.

Following an opening chapter describing the training available to naval aviators to the end of World War I, this chronological narrative devotes two chapters to the first part of the interwar period. The final chapter discusses events during the years from 1934 to 1939, which was a period of considerable expansion for naval aviation. Because of this expansion, the development of more extensive training programs became necessary. Among the numerous topics covered in each chapter are the training programs for both officers and enlisted personnel, the type of training provided, and the programs available at various facilities, including the Naval Academy and the Naval Air Stations at Hampton Roads, San Diego, and Pensacola.

The author of Chapter I of the volume was Lieutenant Commander Clifford L. Lord, USNR, while the other chapters were prepared by Lieutenant (junior grade) George M. Fennemore, USNR. Both authors document their work with extensive footnotes. Lieutenant Fennemore presents commentaries on his sources at the end of each chapter.

34. Office of the Deputy Chief of Naval Operations (Air), "Aviation Training, 1940-1945." Vol. XIV. Washington. n.d. 258 pp.

The second volume of the series on aviation training is a collection of individual studies of various facets of the World War II program. The first focuses on the administration of the wartime air training program. Such aspects as organizational developments, supervision of aviation technical schools, and the establishment of the Naval Air Training Command are discussed.

Some of the remaining studies are more narrow in scope. These include an outline of the achievement testing program used in training pilots and an account of the special training devices program. Basic technical training for inexperienced personnel is another subject covered. A comprehensive summary of Marine aviation training is presented in the final paper.

Several authors prepared these studies. Lieutenant (junior grade) George M. Fennemore, USNR, was the author of the first three. The fourth was contributed by Lieutenant Commander Moreau B. Chambers, USNR, while the final study was written by First Lieutenant Ann F. Vaupel, USMC (WR).

35. Office of the Deputy Chief of Naval Operations (Air), "The Civil Aeronautics Administration-War Training Service (Navy) Flight Training Program." Vol. XV. Washington. n.d. 75 pp., appendices.

The Navy's utilization of the pilot training program of the Civil Aeronautics Administration (earlier known as the Civil Aeronautics Authority) is described in this volume. The CAA program of aviation training in colleges, universities, and flying schools throughout the country, as well as the effort to produce military pilots within the agency's existing civilian administration system, is discussed in the first chapter. The increased demand for military pilots necessitated considerable expansion of this program betwen 1939 and 1944.

Chapter II examines the Navy's part in coordinating the project and evaluates the attempt to restructure civilian pilot training to meet the particular needs of naval aviation. The use of CAA facilities from 1942 to 1944 for the Navy's program of reducing the time needed for flight training is focused on in the third chapter. Chapter IV is devoted to problems encountered in the assignment of naval personnel, standardization of training requirements, supervision and inspection of training activities, and the loss of civilian instructors.

The appendices contain several statistical tables related to cost, manpower usage, and the number of individuals trained.

36.   Office of the Deputy Chief of Naval Operations (Air), "Aviation in the Fleet Exercies, 1911-1939." Vol. XVI. Washington. n.d. 231 pp.

This volume examines each of the major fleet exercises conducted between 1911 and 1939 and evaluates their contribution to the development of naval aviation. The problems, limitations, and successes of the operations are depicted. A concise summary of fleet exercises appears on pages 221-228.

37.   Office of the Deputy Chief of Naval Operations (Air), "Procurement of Naval Aircraft, 1907-1939." Vol. XVII. Washington. 1946. 376 pp., appendices.

This is the first of three monographs prepared by the Office of the Deputy Chief of Naval Operations (Air) that deal with the procurement of naval aircraft.

After a brief summary of early aviation activities, the narrative reviews procurement efforts by the Navy from the first appropriation for aviation in 1911 through the start of World War I. The following section examines lighter-than-air craft and balloons. This section includes three appendices containing cost estimates, airship specifications, and excerpts from congressional appropriation hearings.

The treatment of procurement during World War I concentrates on such topics as the state of the aircraft industry at the time, the acceleration of aircraft production, and the difficulties of procurement organization and administration. Coverage of the interwar period considers the changes in procurement procedures that resulted from the establishment of the Bureau of Aeronautics in 1921. The final section discusses the legal technicalities that the Bureau of Aeronautics faced in its procurement activities after the passage of the Aircraft Procurement Act of 1926.

The author of the history was Lieutenant Commander William O. Shanahan, USNR.

38. Office of the Deputy Chief of Naval Operations (Air), "Aviation Procurement, 1939-1945." Vols. XVIII and XIX. Washington. 1946. 830 pp., appendices.

These two volumes contain ten separate narratives dealing with the accelerated procurement of naval aircraft between 1939 and 1945.

In Part I of the first volume, the administrative control of procurement and production within the Bureau of Aeronautics is characterized. The second part of the volume describes the administrative activities related to the procurement of government-furnished equipment. The acquisition of aviation spare parts and subcontracting are discussed in Parts III and IV, respectively, while the role of the Office of Procurement and Material in coordinating and reviewing procurement, and in providing policy guidance, is considered in the fifth part. The history of the Inspection Division from its establishment in 1921 is dealt with in Part VI, with emphasis placed on the expansion experienced during 1939-1945.

The second volume begins with a history of Army-Navy cooperation in aircraft procurement and details the establishment of requirements, production scheduling, contract regulations, competition for resources, and design and development standardization. Aid to Allied governments within the framework of lend-lease agreements is covered in the second part of the volume, while the third deals with the procurement of such special devices as radar equipment. Part IV discusses the administration of the security program for personnel in factories manufacturing classified material.

Most of the individual sections of the two volumes include appendices containing basic policy directives and copies of forms used to administer the procurement effort. The various sections were written by Lieutenant Commander W. O. Shanahan, USNR, and Lieutenants D. A. Bergmark, USNR, A. R. Buchanan, USNR, and George Tobias, USNR.

39. Office of the Deputy Chief of Naval Operations (Air), "The Navy's Transport Glider Program, 1941-1943." Vol. XX. Washington. 1944. 530 pp., appendix.

In this monograph, the history of the transport glider program is presented as a case study in aviation procurement. The volume begins with a listing of the extensive records that were examined by the author and a concise summary of the volume. The basic narrative is divided into three parts, the first of which is a comprehensive chronological history of the glider program. The second part evaluates the role of individual aeronautical contractors in the glider program. Part III is a detailed cost accounting of the project.

The remainder of the volume consists of an appendix containing fifty-one exhibits. This material includes articles, reports, letters, directives, and memoranda. A number of blueprints and photographs of gliders also appear in this section. The author of the study was Lieutenant (junior grade) Robert Vance Brown, USNR.

40. Office of the Deputy Chief of Naval Operations (Air), "Aviation Personnel, 1911-1939." Vol. XXI. Washington. n.d. 407 pp.

This well documented volume is divided into three distinct parts, each representing a phase in the chronological history of the administration of naval aviation personnel prior to World War II. Part I, the shortest section, deals with the period before World War I, when naval aviation was in its infancy. The second part is a chronological account of developments relating to aviation personnel between 1911 and 1933. The contents deal primarily with the World War I and postwar period, and emphasis is placed on the establishment of the various aviation enlisted ratings. The years from 1934 to 1939 are described in Part III. Included are accounts of the administrative effort to supplement aviation personnel through the Naval Reserve system and the use of enlisted pilots.

Lieutenant Taulman A. Miller, USNR, prepared Parts I and III, while Lieutenant Commander Richard M. Carrigan, USNR, wrote Part II.

41.   Office of the Deputy Chief of Naval Operations (Air), "Aviation Personnel, 1939-1945." Vol. XXII. Washington. n.d. 487 pp.

This volume is concerned with the administration of naval aviation personnel between 1939 and 1945. The first section focuses on the period of limited national emergency from 1939 to 1941. The second, covering the war years, provides a history of administrative activities involved in increasing the number of qualified aviation personnel, rotating personnel in combat, maintaining training standards, and collecting data for the formulation and operation of the program.

An historical account and appraisal of statistical control methods employed by the Personnel Division of the Office of the Deputy Chief of Naval Operations (Air) is included in the third section. The discussion furnishes insight into the administrative relationships with the Bureau of Naval Personnel and other commands. Following the narrative is a biographical note discussing source material utilized in the preparation of the volume.

Lieutenant Taulman A. Miller, USNR, was the author of the first two sections, and Lieutenant Commander Robert C. Weems, Jr., USNR, contributed the section on statistical controls.

42.   Office of the Deputy Chief of Naval Operations (Air), "Air Task Organization in the Pacific Ocean Areas: Task Organization of Ship-Based Aircraft." Washington. n.d. 509 pp.

This volume outlines the organization of ship-based aircraft in the Pacific during World War II. For the period from December 1941 to September 1944, the text is divided into geographic sections covering operations in the North, South, Central, and Southwest Pacific.

The remainder of the text includes sections for the Philippines, Iwo Jima, and Okinawa campaigns during late 1944 and 1945. Besides providing an overall picture of the naval air units assigned to operations, each section lists specific aviation units involved and the ships in which the aircraft were based.

The compilers were Lieutenants Andrew R. Hile, Jr., USNR, Merrill E. Jarchow, USNR, and Rose L. Golden, USNR.

43. Office of the Deputy Chief of Naval Operations (Air), "Air Task Organization in Pacific Ocean Areas: Task Organization of Land-Based Aircraft." Washington. n.d. 352 pp.

The units comprising land-based air task forces in the Pacific during World War II are listed in this volume. The work is organized by geographical areas, with sections covering the North, South, Central, and Western Pacific, the Hawaiian Sea Frontier, the Marshall-Gilbert Islands, and the West Coast of the United States. Each section identifies those land-based aircraft units operating within a given task force at any given time.

The compilers include Lieutenant Commander Henry M. Dater, USNR, and Lieutenants Rose L. Golden, USNR, Robert W. July, USNR, and Adrian O. Van Wyen, USNR.

44. Office of the Deputy Chief of Naval Operations (Air), "The Development of Fleet Air Wings." Washington. 1946. 877 pp., appendices.

Part I of this volume begins with a narrative summary of the development of the administrative organization of the air wings, the basic organizational units for land-based fleet aircraft. The development of special functions and the expansion of the wings during World War II also are discussed. Appendices contain organizational data, a chronology of significant dates, and copies of selected dispatches.

The second part consists of excerpts from the histories of Fleet Air Wings 1, 3, 4, 14, 16, 17, and Group One (FAW-17). The author of the narrative was Lieutenant A. O. Van Wyen, USNR.

45. Office of the Deputy Chief of Naval Operations (Air), "Air Task Organization in the Atlantic Ocean Area." Washington. 1945. 198 pp.

This compilation outlines the organization of air task forces assigned to specific sea frontiers, European waters, and the South Atlantic. An added section on the United States Fleet covers escort carrier task forces and aviation components based at Newfoundland, Greenland, and Iceland. Each of the geographic sections is divided into time periods. According to the preface of the volume, this reconstruction of air task organization in the Atlantic Area is based on operation plans and orders, supplemented by war diaries and unit histories.

Lieutenant Jay Du Von, USNR, and Lieutenant John P. King, USNR, were the compilers.

Commandant, United States Marine Corps

46. Office of the Commandant, U. S. Marine Corps, "United States Marine Corps." Washington. 1946. 449 pp., appendices.

 Divided into five parts, this history methodically discusses all aspects of the administration of the Marine Corps in World War II. The narrative begins with a brief prologue providing an overview of command structure, personnel procurement and training, and logistical problems. The second part outlines the organizational structure and functions of the various divisions of Marine Corps Headquarters, including personnel, quartermaster, paymaster, plans and policies, and aviation. Of the two parts that follow, the first deals with the Department of the Pacific, which was responsible for most Marine activities in the Eleventh, Twelfth, Fifteenth, and Seventeenth Naval Districts, while the second describes the wartime operation of Camp Lejeune, North Carolina. Part V, containing twelve chapters, is a lengthy explanation of the administration of the Fleet Marine Force, Pacific. Such aspects as command responsibilities, training, procurement of personnel, and administrative relationships with other commands are examined in detail.

 Included with the general administrative history is an additional narrative section, designated Annex A, that traces the development and operation of the Marine Corps Women's Reserve from 1943 to 1945. Accompanying this lengthy annex is an appendix listing sources used in the preparation of this section of the history.

Bureau of Aeronautics

47.   Bureau of Aeronautics, "Summary." 2 vols. Washington. 1957. 1,268 pp., appendix, index.

These volumes present a summary of the twenty-volume administrative history of the Bureau of Aeronautics that covers the period July 1939 to June 1947. The first bound volume is a synopsis of Volumes I, III, IV through VIII, and X of the basic series, while the second summarizes Volumes II, IX, and XI through XX. The overall administrative history was prepared by personnel of the Technical Services Corporation under a contract with the bureau. The authors of the two summary volumes were Carl Berger and Dr. Mapheus Smith.

48.   Bureau of Aeronautics, "Background." Vol. I. Washington. 1957. 232 pp., chronology, appendix, index.

The prewar history of the Bureau of Aeronautics is presented in this volume. Among the topics treated are the origins and development of naval aviation, the establishment of the Bureau of Aeronautics, the role of the American aircraft industry, and congressional actions related to naval aviation. In addition, the bureau's research programs, internal organization, relationships with other organizations, and aspects of personnel and training are discussed.

The work is well documented. Together with other volumes in the series, it includes an excellent chronology of major events. Two basic documents on the establishment of the bureau are located in the appendix. The first draft of the volume was prepared jointly by Ashley F. Davis, Norman R. Pyle, and William F. Reinke. A revised draft was prepared by Bee Stockton and edited by Dr. Mapheus Smith.

49.   Bureau of Aeronautics, "Organization and Administration." Vol. II. Washington. 1957. 331 pp., chronology, appendix, index.

An overall summary of the organization and functions of the Bureau of Aeronautics during 1939 - 1947 is provided in this volume. The study begins with an examination of the divisional organization of the bureau. Subsequent discussion covers the reorganization of the entire activity in 1941 as a result of the management study conducted by Booz, Fry, Allen, and Hamilton; the transfer of planning and other important functions to the Deputy Chief of Naval Operations (Air) in 1943; the establishment of the Integrated Aeronautic Program; and the bureau's reorganization in 1946. In addition, the narrative reviews the administration of several maintenance programs of the bureau, such as those dealing with management improvement, equipment and office supply, communications, and security.

The appendix includes 225 pages of key documents, the bulk of which were originated by the Bureau of Aeronautics and the Deputy Chief of Naval Operations (Air). The volume was prepared initially by Bee Stockton. It was rewritten and edited by Dr. Mapheus Smith.

50.   Bureau of Aeronautics, "Operational Responsibilities." Vol. III. Washington. 1957. 142 pp., chronology, appendix, index.

The narrative begins with a general treatment of the background and extent of the bureau's operational responsibilities and the events leading to the transfer, in August 1943, of most of these duties to the Deputy Chief of Naval Operations (Air). Examples of the wide scope of responsibilities included the organization and assignment of aviation operational units and the transportation of naval aircraft within the United States. The bureau's relationships with other organizations regarding operational policy and duties also are discussed.

Important memoranda and organizational documents are included in the appendix. The first draft of the study was prepared by Bee Stockton. It subsequently was rewritten and edited by Dr. Mapheus Smith.

51. Bureau of Aeronautics, "Determination of Military Characteristics." Vol. IV. Washington. 1957. 95 pp., chronology, appendix, index.

The organizational arrangements and procedures employed in the determination of military characteristics of naval aircraft and of aeronautical equipment are described in this brief but well documented narrative. It also outlines the continuous process by which changes in characteristics were made throughout the war years. Among the specific examples discussed were the determination of characteristics in regard to torpedo bombers, scout planes, armor, and compasses.

The appendix includes a number of memoranda pertaining to military requirements policy and other pertinent documentation. The author of the volume was Dr. Mapheus Smith.

52.   Bureau of Aeronautics, "Aviation Planning." Vol. V. Washington. 1957. 318 pp., chronology, appendix, index.

This history places special emphasis on the planning of aircraft production and the allocation of aircraft to perform specialized functions. Among the topics discussed in the first five chapters of the narrative are the establishment of formal planning procedures during World War II; the reassignment of planning functions when the Office of the Deputy Chief of Naval Operations (Air) was established in August 1943; and the subsequent steps taken by the Bureau of Aeronautics to build its own planning organization. The final chapter focuses on postwar planning developments.

The extensive appendix contains copies of directives, plans, and reports. The author of the study was Dr. Mapheus Smith.

53.   Bureau of Aeronautics, "Procurement, Production and Contracts." Vol. VI and "Appendix Documents -- Procurement, Production and Contracts." Vol. VI (A). Washington. 1957. 584 pp., chronology, appendix, index.

The procurement and production programs of the Bureau of Aeronautics during the interwar period and World War II are evaluated in this volume. Information is included on the status of the aircraft industry, manpower difficulties, the related activities of other government organizations, and the bureau's policies and procedures that affected its procurement and production functions. Major emphasis is placed on the organization of the bureau in these fields and its record of accomplishment during the war years. Contracting policies and procedures are discussed in broad terms, with considerable detail presented on certain key decisions.

A separate appendix volume contains numerous memoranda, reports, charts, and organizational diagrams related to topics dealt with in the text. The first draft of the work was prepared by Norman R. Pyle. Dr. Mapheus Smith reorganized and edited the final manuscript.

54. Bureau of Aeronautics, "Naval Aviation Inspection." Vol. VII. Washington. 1957. 141 pp., chronology, appendix, index.

The organization, policy, procedures, and problems of the Bureau of Aeronautics in inspecting aircraft and aeronautical material during the wartime production process are analyzed in this volume. The cooperation of the bureau with the Army Air Force and other organizations in regard to inspection also is evaluated.

Several important memoranda and reports, and an organizational diagram, are included in the appendix. The narrative was written by Norman R. Pyle and edited by Dr. Mapheus Smith.

55. Bureau of Aeronautics, "Maintenance." Vol. VIII. Washington. 1957. 246 pp., chronology, appendix, index.

A detailed discussion of programs concerned with assembly, repair, maintenance, and overhaul of aircraft and aeronautical equipment, implemented by the Bureau of Aeronautics both in Washington and in the field, is provided in this volume. The administrative structure, policy decisions, procedures, and accomplishments of these programs are detailed. Special attention is given to the planning and review aspects of maintenance.

Over half of the volume consists of appendix documents. Key letters, memoranda, and orders are located in this section. The study was prepared by Carl Berger and edited by Dr. Mapheus Smith.

56. Bureau of Aeronautics, "Material and Supply." Vol. IX. Washington. 1957. 251 pp., chronology, appendix, index.

This narrative examines the contribution of the Bureau of Aeronautics to aviation supply during World War II and the bureau's postwar efforts to prepare for future national emergencies. To a considerable extent, the discussion focuses on the bureau's cooperation with other organizations in supplying aeronautical material for use by the Navy. Such agencies included the Bureau of Supplies and Accounts, Aviation Supply Office, the Bureau of Ordnance, and the Deputy Chief of Naval Operations (Air).

Among the extensive appendices are various letters and other documents originated by the Bureau of Aeronautics as well as by other organizations associated with aviation supply. The author of the narrative was Carl Berger. Final editing was undertaken by Dr. Mapheus Smith.

57. Bureau of Aeronautics, "Research, Technical Developments, and Engineering." Vol. X. Washington. 1957. 419 pp., chronology, appendix, index.

Following a brief description of the prewar research and development functions of the Bureau of Aeronautics, this history reviews some of the administrative aspects of these programs during World War II. The narrative presents a general account of the bureau's accomplishments related to the many types of aircraft, power plants, and aeronautical equipment needed by the Navy during the war. Much of the material for this history was derived from a ten-volume report on the bureau's research and development activities that was prepared for a Senate investigation of the national defense program in 1945.

An appendix includes numerous key letters, memoranda, and orders, in addition to several charts. The first version of this manuscript was completed by Carl Charlic. Carl Berger prepared the second version, which subsequently was edited by Dr. Mapheus Smith.

58. Bureau of Aeronautics, "Aviation Shore Establishments." Vol. XI. Washington. 1957. 319 pp., chronology, appendix, index.

The part played by the Bureau of Aeronautics in developing and administering aviation shore establishments during World War II, and in the demobilization period immediately following the war, is discussed in this volume. Considerable attention is given to the bureau's overall planning of air bases and to changes in the number and type of planes assigned to these facilities.

Principal sources used in writing the narrative included "Aviation Shore Establishment, 1911-1945," one of the administrative history volumes prepared for the office of the Deputy Chief of Naval Operations (Air); and the World War II administrative history of the Bureau of Yards and Docks. Copies of other official documentary sources that were utilized are located in a lengthy appendix section. Among these are various directives, reports, and tables. The authors of the volume were Ashley F. Davis, Norman R. Pyle, William Reinke, and

Dr. Mapheus Smith.

59. Bureau of Aeronautics, "Aviation Personnel and Training." Vol. XII. Washington. 1957. 399 pp., chronology, appendix, index.

Divided into three parts, this history reviews the administration of personnel by the Bureau of Aeronautics and the fulfillment of the bureau's training responsibilities. The first part focuses on the organization's own military and civilian personnel. Part II deals with the bureau's administrative activities related to other personnel involved in naval aviation, and Part III examines training responsibilities. Both of these overall functions ended in August 1943 when such activities were transferred to the newly established Office of the Deputy Chief of Naval Operations (Air).

Much of the material in this volume is taken from the personnel and training volumes in the administrative history series of the Deputy Chief of Naval Operations (Air). The forty pages of appendix documents are divided into three parts, corresponding with the text, and include directives pertaining to personnel qualifications and charts indicating personnel strengths at different periods during the war. The volume's author was Norman R. Pyle.

60. Bureau of Aeronautics, "Budget Planning and Administration." Vol. XIII. Washington. 1957. 265 pp., chronology, appendix, index.

This narrative deals with the process by which the Bureau of Aeronautics obtained operating funds and the policies and procedures followed in administering these funds. In discussing the first of these aspects, detailed accounts are given of all appropriation bills for each fiscal year during the war, showing the steps involved in evaluating budget needs and in requesting and obligating funds for each major subdivision of naval aviation. The bureau's administration of the budget is presented as a chronological analysis divided into two chapters, one covering the war years and the other the postwar period through 1947.

The appendix section contains copies of key directives and orders, a glossary of terminology used in financial planning, and a number of statistical tables. Dr. Mapheus Smith and Norman R. Pyle prepared the volume.

61. Bureau of Aeronautics, "Naval Aviation Photography and Motion Pictures." Vol. XIV. Washington. 1957. 128 pp., chronology, appendix, index.

The role of the Bureau of Aeronautics in the field of aviation photography during World War II is outlined in this volume. Among the topics covered are the procedures and problems related to administering the bureau's photographic division; the expansion and operation of training programs for photographers, photographic interpretation specialists, and other photographic technicians; and accomplishments in development, procurement, and supply of photographic equipment and material. The bureau's part in military photography, including intelligence applications, also is discussed. The training film program and film cataloging activities are examined.

Appendix documents, occupying about half

of the volume, consist of copies of twenty-two directives, memoranda, and reports. Granville W. Dutton submitted the first draft of this history, while the final manuscript was rewritten and edited by Dr. Mapheus Smith.

62. Bureau of Aeronautics, "Aerology." Vol. XV. Washington. 1957. 81 pp., chronology, appendix, index.

This study briefly describes the administration of the Navy's aerological program by the Bureau of Aeronautics. The discussion focuses on the bureau's role in the development, support, and operation of the aerological service. Although planning, policy making, and operational responsibilities for aerology were transferred to the Office of the Deputy Chief of Naval Operations (Air) in 1943, the bureau continued to have budgetary, research, procurement, supply, and maintenance responsibilities. Besides examining administrative aspects of the aerological program, the narrative considers research efforts that were undertaken, including relationships with other government organizations engaged in climatological and meteorological studies.

Fourteen documents related to the aerological program are included in the appendix. Dr. Mapheus Smith was the author of the volume.

63. Bureau of Aeronautics, "Publications." Vol. XVI. Washington. 1957. 143 pp., chronology, appendix, index.

A concise history of the general and technical publication program of the Bureau of Aeronautics during World War II is presented in this volume. Such aspects as organizational and administrative arrangements, Army-Navy coordination, procurement, reproduction, distribution, indexing, forms control, and field liaison are discussed.

Copies of various directives, letters, and memoranda constitute the appendix section of the volume. The authors were Ashley F. Davis and Dr. Mapheus Smith.

64.   Bureau of Aeronautics, "Foreign Aid." Vol. XVII. Washington. 1957. 119 pp., chronology, appendix, index.

A history of the wartime activities of the Bureau of Aeronautics in aiding Allied nations is presented in this work. This program operated under the auspices of lend-lease and was part of the Navy's extensive effort to provide material assistance in the war against the Axis powers. The narrative covers the background of foreign aid, describes lend-lease operations, and includes a chronological outline of the bureau's administration of defense aid betwen 1941 and 1945.

Along with copies of directives and instructions, organizational charts and statistical tables related to the bureau's foreign aid effort are included in the appendix. The history was prepared by Norman R. Pyle and edited by Dr. Mapheus Smith.

65.   Bureau of Aeronautics, "Aviation Medicine." Vol. XVIII. Washington. 1957. 77 pp., chronology, appendix, index.

This manuscript presents a review of the organization and activities of the Bureau of Aeronautics in the field of aviation medicine during the war and in the immediate postwar period. An account of some of the most important accomplishments to which the bureau made a contribution also is included. Among the topics treated in the narrative are the bureau's involvement in oxygen, high altitude, and vision research; in studies of the effects of acceleration, deceleration, impact, and noise; in investigation of fatigue and stimulants; and in the development of suitable uniforms for aviation personnel.

Most of the appendix documents are reports of medical research undertaken by the bureau. The authors were Granville W. Dutton and Dr. Mapheus Smith.

66. Bureau of Aeronautics, "Air Intelligence." Vol. XIX. Washington. 1957. 82 pp., chronology, appendix, index.

Following an explanation of the operational and technical aspects of naval air intelligence, this narrative examines the contribution of the Bureau of Aeronautics to these intelligence programs during World War II. The first part of the discussion deals with operational intelligence from 1940 until 1943, when this function was tranferred to the Deputy Chief of Naval Operations (Air). The remainder of the narrative is devoted to an analysis of the bureau's use of technical intelligence during the war years.

The appendix includes a variety of documents related to both the operational and technical facets of intelligence. The first draft of this study was prepared by Granville W. Dutton. This was revised by Norman R. Pyle and edited by Dr. Mapheus Smith.

67.   Bureau of Aeronautics, "Marine Corps Aviation." Vol. XX. Washington. 1957. 100 pp., chronology, appendix, index.

The relationship of the Bureau of Aeronautics with Headquarters, U. S. Marine Corps, and the means by which the bureau provide material support for Marine Corps aviation, are discussed in this history. Management and training of Marine Corps aviation personnel also are covered.

Several memoranda and organizational charts are located in the appendix. The authors of the volume were Bee Stockton and Dr. Mapheus Smith.

Bureau of Medicine and Surgery

68.   Bureau of Medicine and Surgery, "The United States Navy Medical Department at War, 1941-1945." Vol. I (bound in 2 vols.). Washington. 1946. 757 pp., appendices.

These volumes describe the operational role of naval medical units ashore and afloat during the war. Part I begins with a discussion of the Medical Department's preparedness prior to Pearl Harbor and its activities during and after the attack. Actions in the Philippines and the Netherlands East Indies are focused upon in the subsequent narrative. The second part, entitled "Allied Offensive in the Pacific," details medical aspects of the campaigns in the Solomons, Aleutians, Gilberts, New Guinea, Marshalls, Marianas, Carolines, and the Philippines. Part III examines events associated with the defeat of Japan, including the Iwo Jima and Okinawa operations, and the beginning of the occupation of Japan. The Allied invasions of North Africa and Europe (Sicily, Salerno, Normandy, and Southern France) are considered in the final part.

The narrative in each part covers planning and training for the various campaigns, activities during amphibious assults, establishment of medical care facilities ashore, methods of supply, medical reports, and sanitation procedures.

Each chapter concludes with a list of source materials. Several chapters also contain appendices covering such subjects as casualty statistics and supply inventories. Numerous photographs are found throughout the volumes. The entire study was a collective effort by a staff of historians and researchers directed by Lieutenant Commander Chester L. Guthrie H(S), USNR. Portions of the manuscript, dealing with major campaigns, were used in Volume I of The History of the Medical Department of the United States Navy in World War II, published by the Government Printing Office in 1953.

69. Bureau of Medicine and Surgery, "The United States Navy Medical Department at War, 1941-1945." Vol. II (bound in 2 vols.). Washington. 1946. 1,045 pp., appendices.

The administration of the Bureau of Medicine and Surgery during the war is the focus of this history. The narrative is divided into four parts, the first of which discusses the organization of the bureau. Besides documenting its wartime expansion, this section includes brief background information tracing developments during the interwar period. Part II examines various bureau functions, including the operation of naval hospitals and dispensaries, as well as various educational and training programs. A summary of the Marine Corps medical program also is presented.

A more detailed consideration of the bureau's activities in the continental United States is provided in the third part. A similar treatment of the same type of activity outside the United States appears in the final section. Such aspects as facility planning, supply of medicine and medical equipment, and the operation of particular medical activities are covered in each of the last two parts.

Most chapters include an indication of published and unpublished materials upon which the narrative was based. In addition, various statistical tables, certain organizational charts, and some reports are included as appendices. A staff of historians and researchers directed by Lieutenant Commander Chester L. Guthrie H(S), USNR, prepared the study. Portions of the history, related to medical facilities, were used in volume I of <u>The History of the Medical Department of the United States in World War II</u>, published by the Government Printing Office in 1953.

Bureau of Ordnance

70. Bureau of Ordnance, "Organization, Administration, and Special Functions." Washington. n.d. 344 pp., appendices.

A general description of the organization and mission of the Bureau of Ordnance during World War II is provided in this volume. The prewar administrative structure of the bureau, its reorganization in 1941, and other wartime measures developed for improved management are detailed. Data are included on office functions, security, bureau publications, and relations with industry and the public. The bureau's relationships with other naval entities, as well as the Army, are considered. The volume concludes with a discussion of the administrative procedures used in coordinating the numerous ordnance establishments under the cognizance of the bureau.

A list of ordnance activities along with several statistical tables and charts are included in the appendices to the volume. An annotated bibliography of bureau publications also is found in this section.

71. Bureau of Ordnance, "Planning." Washington. n.d. 228 pp.,

This study focuses on the work of the Planning and Progress Division of the Bureau of Ordnance between 1941 and 1945. A thorough discussion of the establishment and functioning of the division's directives system provides insight into the administrative machinery designed to initiate and carry out the bureau's programs. Also included is an analysis of the effort to provide statistical data essential to planning activities. The bureau's important role in the lend-lease program is treated in a separate section of the narrative. Various statistics, such as a detailed breakdown of expenditures for ordnance materials supplied through lend-lease, are provided in this section. Key documents are included as appendices.

72. Bureau of Ordnance, "Procurement." Washington. n.d. 237 pp., appendices.

The procurement organization and activities of the Production Division of the Bureau of Ordnance are detailed in this volume. The narrative begins in 1933, but concentrates on the immediate prewar and war years. Considerable detail is presented on purchasing procedures, as well as the various types of contracts employed. A chapter of procurement statistics outlines costs by item and year. The contributions of specific personnel involved in these programs are noted throughout the study.

Organizational charts are included in the text. In addition, six appendices provide supplementary discussions of such subjects as the ordnance inspection service of the bureau and the procurement of machine tools and facilities.

73. Bureau of Ordnance, "Research and Development, Maintenance." Washington. n.d. 373 pp., appendices.

This volume contains two sections. The first examines the wartime administrative structure and activities of the Research and Development Division of the Bureau of Ordnance. Specific functions of several offices within the division are discussed, including those of the Design Group, the Ship Characteristics and Fleet Requirements Subsection, and the Ammunition Quality Evaluation Unit. Topics reviewed include supervision of research activities and contracts, patent administration, packaging and materials handling, and analysis of foreign ordnance.

The second section of the volume is an administrative history of the bureau's Maintenance Division. The narrative emphasizes the disposition and supply of ordnance equipment and material, which was one of the most important functions of the division. Details also are presented on other activities, including the allocation of aviation ordnance, ordnance allowances, and repairs and alterations. Information regarding demobilization and postwar ordnance planning is provided in the final pages of the text. A series of organizational charts appears in the appendices.

74. Bureau of Ordnance, "Personnel and Training, Finance, Special Board, Legal Counsel." Washington. n.d. 263 pp., appendices.

Several aspects of the wartime operation of the Bureau of Ordnance are presented in the five separate parts of this volume. The first part begins by discussing the assignment of large numbers of qualified officers and men to meet the bureau's expanded staff requirements in Washington and in the field. Among the subsequent topics covered are the allocation, classification, training, promotion, and demobilization of personnel. For the most part, the appendices relate to training programs, although one statistical table shows the increase in the number of officers assigned to the bureau from 1918 to 1945.

An analysis of the organization and administration of civilian manpower employed by the bureau is provided in the second section. Part III reviews the wartime activities of the bureau's Financial Division. That office was responsible for securing, allocating, and regulating the use of funds. The development of allocation procedures for both regular and lend-lease appropriations is detailed. Monthly status reports reflecting estimates and expenditures for all types of ordnance in 1945 are located among the appendices. Also included are an organizational chart; summaries of the bureau's investment in land, buildings, and equipment; and a table showing yearly appropriations from 1939 to 1946.

The activities and composition of the

Special Board on Naval Ordnance are reviewed briefly in the fourth part. This group of senior officers dealt with technical programs and policies that extended across organizational lines within the bureau. The final section of the narrative summarizes the wartime role of the bureau's Office of Counsel.

75. Bureau of Ordnance, "Guns and Mounts." Washington. n.d. 290 pp., appendices.

Following a brief introduction, each of the twelve basic chapters of this study examines the development, production, and distribution of a specific type of weapon used by the Navy in World War II. Among the ordnance discussed are machine, antiaircraft, 3-inch, 5-inch, 6-inch, 8-inch, 12-inch, and 16-inch guns, as well as small arms. In addition to providing much technical data, the commentary on each weapon details the prewar and wartime history of its use. Efforts to increase production and improve efficiency of particular weapons are recounted. Various factors involved in the procurement and placement of heavy guns on board ships also are considered. Closely related to this subject is the review made of the development and employment of mounts for different ordnance items. The appendices include key correspondence, sample procurement contracts, and brief historical summaries of certain topics.

76. Bureau of Ordnance, "Armor, Projectiles, Ammunition Details, Bombs and Plastics." Washington. 436 pp., appendices.

Divided into five parts, this work examines the development, production, and allocation of specific ordnance items. The first part focuses on the revitalization of the dormant armor industry at the beginning of World War II. Problems confronted in expanding manufacturing facilities are analyzed. Aspects of armor research and development also are covered. The subsequent section on projectiles deals with efforts to coordinate production to meet Army, Navy, and Allied needs. Among the difficulties that had to be overcome was the procurement of adequate quantities of armor-piercing projectiles at a time when only a few contractors had experience in the field.

Development and manufacture of fuzes is the primary emphasis of the section concerning ammunition. The discussion details the history of various types of fuzes used during the war. In addition, the production of cartridge cases, powder tanks, and other containers is treated. A descriptive list of all wartime fuze types, contractors, and quantities produced are included in the appendices to the section.

Bomb procurement and manufacture is the subject of the fourth part of the volume. Army-Navy efforts to standardize bomb requirements also are outlined. The appendices to the section provide detailed statistical tables on production quantities and types of bombs. The final section examines experimentation and utilization of plastics for ordnance purposes. Ammunition, bomb racks, batteries, cartridge cases, gauges, gun mounts, mines, rockets, and torpedoes were among the numerous items for which plastics were tested.

77.   Bureau of Ordnance, "Rockets, Explosives and Propellants, Pyrotechnics." Washington. n.d. 429 pp., appendix.

This volume follows a format similar to that of the others in the series by focusing on particular weapons and devices. The first part of the narrative details the administration and operation of the rocket program under the Bureau of Ordnance. A brief history of rocket development and concise descriptions of the various types of rockets used during World War II are presented. Several statistical tables and charts showing rocket production follow the narrative. The appendix accompanying this section provides concise histories of several types of rocket launchers.

The second part of the volume outlines the general history of explosive ordnance and its employment during the war. Discussions are included on research and development efforts involving explosives and propellants, wartime production activities, and the transportation facilities and techniques developed for such material. The final narrative section reviews the development, production, and use of pyrotechnics such as flares, signals, and markers.

78. Bureau of Ordnance, "Underwater Ordnance." Washington. n.d. 473 pp., appendices.

The five sections of this volume examine the equipment developed by the Bureau of Ordnance for use in underwater warfare. The opening section deals with degaussing devices and techniques used to reduce magnetic fields around ships so as to protect them from magnetically detonated mines and torpedoes. Topics covered include the design and installation of equipment, as well as the procurement and training of personnel involved in degaussing.

Mine development and production is the subject of the second part of the volume. A summary of the offensive mining of Japanese home waters is included in this section. The following part is devoted to booms and nets, including those used to protect harbors and individual ships and submarines. The wartime employment of depth charges is treated in part four. Various types of charges are described in turn. A review of depth charge launching devices concludes the section.

The final section focuses on torpedoes. Besides covering production and maintenance of torpedoes and torpedo launching gear, the narrative provides historical and technical information on this weapon. Several appendices contain statistical data on the ordnance discussed in the test.

79. Bureau of Ordnance, "Fire Control (Except Radar) and Aviation Ordnance." Washington. n.d. 308 pp., appendices.

The first part of this narrative discusses the intensive research and development in fire control, undertaken prior to and during World War II, and the production of fire control devices by commercial contractors. The coverage includes the general fire control systems used on board ships, and specialized equipment for underwater ordnance and antiaircraft weapons.

The second section of the volume focuses on aviation ordnance, including its associated fire control equipment. Much emphasis is placed on the development and production of various types of ordnance such as aircraft guns, guided missiles, bomb racks, and smoke equipment. Several memoranda and reports on fire control and aviation ordance are located in the lengthy section of appendices.

Bureau of Naval Personnel

80.   Bureau of Naval Personnel, "Preface: Structure of the Bureau." 4 vols. Washington. 1946. 461 pp., appendices.

      The first section of this history is a brief summary of the entire series of administrative histories of the Bureau of Naval Personnel. A list of the authors involved in the project is included.

      An outline of the organization and responsibilities of the bureau's numerous divisions in presented in the second section. The opening chapter presents a helpful review of the bureau's operations between the World Wars and an analysis of major organizational changes during World War II. The ensuing chapters briefly survey much of what is detailed at greater length in subsequent volumes. A substantial bibliography of both unpublished and published source materials follows the text.

      Three volumes of appendices accompany this study. Numerous directives related to organization, policy, and procedure are found in the first volume, while the second contains a series of organizational charts. The final volume is a copy of a management study by Booz, Fry, Allen, and Hamilton surveying the personnel of the bureau. This history was prepared by Specialist Second Class Henry Beers, USNR.

81.   Bureau of Naval Personnel, "Planning and Control Activity." 2 vols. Washington. 1946. 493 pp., appendices.

      Various aspects of the wartime administration of the Bureau of Naval Personnel's Planning and Control Activity are considered in this volume. Among the key responsibilities of the activity were the development of general personnel policies and the preparation of manpower plans, both of which were undertaken by its Plans and Operations Division. The work of this division is treated in the first section of narrative. Besides detailing its internal organization, the discussion covers the relations of the Plans and Operations Division with field activities.

The second section of the history deals with the Finance and Material Division, which administered the bureau's finances and the allocation of material. Among topics examined are the division's preparation of the bureau's budget, handling of appropriations, and liaison with other units within the Navy Department. The relationship of the Office of the Bureau Counsel to the division's fiscal section is reviewed briefly at the end of the narrative. The counsel's office was established primarily to assist in the drafting, negotiation, and administration of contracts for training naval personnel at non-Navy institutions.

A brief bibliography of unpublished and published source material is found at the end of the volume. In addition, personnel who were interviewed in connection with the history are listed. The separate volume of appendices includes several significant memoranda, as well as a wide variety of reports and bulletins prepared by the various elements within the Planning and Control Activity. The author of this history was Lieutenant Willard Hurst, USNR.

82. Bureau of Naval Personnel, "Officer Personnel." 4 vols. Washington. 1945. 365 pp., appendices.

Three histories of key divisions of the Bureau of Naval Personnel are included in this volume. The first concerns the Officer Procurement Division, which was responsible for the selection of officer candidates. The narrative focuses on organization and operations, including the activities of two of the division's major field offices at New Orleans, Louisiana, and Chicago, Illinois. Along with two volumes of procurement directives, a study evaluating factors involved in the selection of officer candidates is provided among the appendices to the history. Lieutenant Willard Hurst, USNR, was the author of this account.

The second history deals with the functioning of the bureau's Officer Distribution Division. That organization classified and assigned officers and prepared duty and transfer orders. In addition, the division arranged the release of officers from the Navy for reasons of hardship. All of these duties are examined in the narrative. A number of important reports, manuals, memoranda, and forms constitute the appendices to the volume and are bound separately. The overall author was Lieutenant Sherman Hayden, USNR.

The work of the Officer Performance Division is detailed in the final history. Besides handling matters related to the promotion, retirement, discharge, and discipline of all naval officers, that office oversaw the collection and review of fitness reports; administered the awarding of decorations, medals, and citations; and had cognizance over matters related to uniforms. It also undertook the compilation and publication of the Navy Register and Reserve Register. Several documents pertaining to the various activities of the division are found in a separately bound appendix. Lieutenant Hayden also prepared this history.

Each of the three studies is followed by a list of persons interviewed as part of the author's research.

83.   Bureau of Naval Personnel, "Training Activity." Vols. I-IV (bound in 7 vols.). Washington. 1946. 1,366 pp., appendices.

This set of volumes details the work of the Bureau of Naval Personnel's Training Activity, which initiated and administered training programs for naval personnel through its various divisions. Volume I discusses operations of the Standards Curriculum Division. That organization planned curricula, prepared training publications and correspondence courses, and determined achievement levels to be attained from various forms of instruction. The activities of the division ranged from the training of instructors to developing skills among illiterate recruits. Besides its other duties, the division undertook the coordination of voluntary educational services for naval personnel and analyzed qualifications derived from training to assist in the assignment of personnel. The author of the history was Lieutenant Dudley Johnson, USNR.

Accompanying Volume I is a separately bound appendix entitled "Personnel Research and Test Development in the Bureau of Naval Personnel," which provides a series of articles outlining the activities of the Standards and Curriculum Division's Test and Research Section. That office operated with assistance from the National Defense Research Committee and the College Entrance Examination Board. Numerous methods of selection, classification, and achievement testing are described in the various articles. The different types of follow-up studies undertaken by the section are discussed. Sample test materials and forms, as well as graphs and statistical compilations, are found throughout the text and in lengthy appendices. Although the articles were prepared by several authors, the editor of the entire volume was Lieutenant Commander Dewey B. Stuit, USNR.

Volume II of the basic series examines both the Field Administration and Quality Control Divisions. The first organization maintained general supervision over numerous specialized and technical schools offering training to officers and enlisted personnel. In addition, it administered a variety of educational programs at universities and other non-naval institutions, assigned students to the numerous schools and programs, and handled student affairs related to housing and other matters. The division also obtained facilities and materials needed to operate training programs and oversaw the Navy-wide physical fitness program. The Quality Control Division was charged with the inspection of all field training activities and liaison with schools connected with the Navy. The history of the Field Administration Division was completed by Lieutenants Russell Siebert and Henry Thoma, USNR. Lieutenant Siebert prepared the study of the Quality Control Division.

A history of the U. S. Naval Training Center at Great Lakes, Illinois, is furnished in a separately bound appendix to Volume II. Following an introduction summarizing the installation's development prior to World War II, several chapters consider such topics as the wartime organization and administration of the command, its recruit training program, and the operation of those service schools located at the center. The final two chapters deal with training black personnel and athletic programs. A group of eight appendices include organization charts, lists of orders and regulations, curriculum outlines, and a copy of the company commander's manual.

Volume III focuses on the Training Aids Division, which planned and prepared audio-visual training aids to be used in Navy courses. Among these were charts, models, posters, and pamphlets. The organization also edited the Naval Training Bulletin that disseminated information on training standards. Besides reviewing the organization's administration of its other activities, the narrative outlines efforts to distribute training devices and training materials prepared by other divisions. Various charts and forms are found throughout the history. The narrative was prepared by officers assigned to the division. Final editing was accomplished by Lieutenant Dudley Johnson, USNR.

Volume IV of the basic narrative presents a history of the Navy's college training or V-12 program. Among the topics discussed are the origins of the V-12 program, its relationship to the War Manpower Commission, the process by which colleges were selected for participation, procurement of qualified personnel for placement in the program, organization of the academic curriculum, and the administrative structure established within the bureau. Three appendices located at the end of the volume include histories of the V-12 program at Dartmouth College and of the College Training Section of the Field Administration Division, as well as an important memorandum on college contract negotiations. In addition, two volumes of V-12 bulletins accompany the history as separately bound appendices.

The four basic histories provide a list of numerous individuals interviewed during the preparation of each study. In some cases, documentary sources also are noted. A considerable quantity of these unbound appendices is located in another collection of the Navy History Division.

84. Bureau of Naval Personnel, "The Negro in the Navy in World War II." Washington. 1947. 103 pp.

The role of black men and women in the Navy during World War II is discussed in this volume. In detailing the expanding opportunities for these personnel, the history examines recruiting practices, training, personnel administration, and duty assignments. Throughout the narrative, accomplishments and problems in the area of integration are evaluated.

A bibliography of documentary material consulted and the names of persons interviewed during the preparation of the study follow the narrative. In addition, over thirty photographs are located throughout the text. This administrative history is one of the major sources for Dennis D. Nelson's <u>The Integration of the Negro into the U. S. Navy</u> (Farrar, Straus and Young, 1951).

85. Bureau of Naval Personnel, "The Welfare Activity." Washington. 1946. 544 pp.

Assigned numerous responsibilities related to welfare, recreation, and entertainment, the Welfare Activity of the Bureau of Naval Personnel was composed of the Special Services, Corrective Services, and Dependents Welfare Divisions, as well as the Informational Services Section. The operations of the latter section are reviewed briefly in the first part of the history. Among its duties was editing <u>All Hands</u> magazine (designated originally as the <u>Bureau of Naval Personnel - Information Bulletin</u>) and <u>Recreation Journal</u>. The section also provided editorial assistance to numerous ship and station newspapers throughout the Navy.

In the second part of the narrative, the Special Services Division is treated. That organization arranged numerous forms of entertainment for naval personnel, coordinated library services, and maintained ship service stores and officer and enlisted messes on shore. The work of the Corrective Services Divisions is discussed in the third part. That division administered the shore patrol and naval prisons.

In a series of twelve separate reports and chronologies, the final section of the history covers the activities of the Dependents Welfare Division. Among these functions were processing applications for the payment of allotments, family allowances, death gratuities, and mustering out pay; notifying relatives of casualties; and assisting the Bureau of Medicine and Surgery in the administrative processing of casualties. In addition, in early 1943, the Division was assigned the responsibility of administering the National Service Life Insurance program for naval personnel.

A partial bibliography appears at the end of the volume.

86.   Bureau of Naval Personnel, "Chaplains' Division; Records and Transportation Activity; Office of Public Information; Administrative Services." Washington. 1946. 178 pp. appendices.

The five separate histories in this volume cover the work of the Chaplains' Corps, Records Division, Transportation Division, Office of Public Information, and administrative service activities of the Bureau of Naval Personnel. The first history begins with an examination of the objectives and organization of the Chaplains' Corps during the war. Discussion of the development of a comprehensive training program, assignment of chaplains, and distribution of religious material follows. The final part of the history outlines the Corps' relationship with various denominations and how ecclesiastical support for its activities was obtained and increased. A bibliography and a complete series of The Chaplain's Newsletter (July 1943-May/June 1945) supplement the narrative.

Histories of the two divisions of the Bureau's Records and Transportation Activity are found in the second and third parts of the volume. Among other topics, the treatment of the Records Division details the development of effective records management and the eventual usage of filing systems based on automated technology. The other division, Transportation, handled arrangements for travel of naval personnel on non-Navy conveyances. Analysis is made of efforts to solve numerous problems related to assuring efficient transport of personnel and their dependents. Also covered is the division's role in demobilization efforts.

In the fourth history, the wartime administration of the office of the Special Assistant and Director of Public Information is reviewed. Emphasis is placed on training officers to handle public relations and on efforts to arrange press and radio coverage of naval events. In addition, the establishment and operation of a function devoted exclusively to processing photographic material for public use is discussed. The final history dealing with Administrative Services is a brief report summarizing administrative responsibilties of various offices of the Bureau.

87.   Bureau of Naval Personnel, "History of the Enlisted Personnel Activity." 2 vols. Washington. 1946. 496 pp., appendices.

This account treats the wartime functioning of the three major subdivisions under the bureau's Director of Enlisted Personnel: enlisted personnel procurement, distribution, and performance.

In the first part, various facets of the procurement process, such as recruitment, voluntary enlistment, and the Selective Service system are discussed, both chronologically and topically. Particular attention is given to the effort to obtain combat aircrewmen, radio technicians, and men for ship repair and construction units.

In Part II, the text discusses the enlisted personnel distribution procedures and the organizational structure that existed prior to the Pearl Harbor Attack and throughout World War II. The subjects covered included personnel selection techniques, shore duty rotation, rating and promotion policies, recruit assignment, training, classification, and special detailing programs.

The final section deals with aspects of enlisted personnel performance, including disciplinary standards and enforcement of discipline, punishment procedures, the administration of discharges, and the initiation, processing, and recording of promotions.

The text contains statistical tables, graphs, and lists of sources used in compiling the history.

The appendix volume consists of recruiting and induction reports, letters, memoranda, rating classifications, plans for improving the classification system, pamphlets, and sample forms and discharge papers.

88. Bureau of Naval Personnel, "History of the Women's Reserve." 2 vols. Washington. 1946. 322 pp., appendices.

These volumes detail the wartime history of naval women, with particular emphasis on their training and contributions to the war effort. The text provides a comprehensive discussion of how the decisions leading to the establishment of the Women's Reserve on 30 July 1942 were formulated in the Navy and in the legislative and executive branches of the government. The organizational evolution of the office of the Director of Women's Reserve within the Bureau of Naval Personnel is described, with a focus on significant problems encountered. Other subjects treated include relationships with other functions in the Navy Department, with naval shore commands, and with the women's organizations of the other services; the procurement and induction of personnel; public relations; the establishment of naval schools and training facilities at various private schools, colleges, and universities; the types of work performed and the ratings and ranks assigned the reservists; the distribution of personnel to installations; housing, discipline, and welfare policies; and a general description of the Women's Reserve in the final two years of war, when the organization achieved its peak wartime efficiency.

The text contains a list of sources and numerous photographs of training facilities and personnel.

The appendices consist of extracts from pertinent legislative documents, administrative instructions, and brief histories of the Midshipmen's School (WR) at Northampton, Massachusetts; the Naval Training Schools at Stillwater, Oklahoma, and Cedar Falls, Iowa; and the Field Administration Division. The authors of the Northampton, Sillwater, and Cedar Fall histories were Lieutenant (junior grade) Louise T. Stockly, (W), USNR; Lieutenant Elizabeth Geen, (W), USNR; and Commander Everette E. Pettee, respectively.

Flow charts, reports, memoranda, letters, site plans, regulations, an officers' roster, conference notes, tables, and graphs, as well as a detailed narrative, comprise the history of the Naval Training School, the Bronx, New York, which is separately bound.

Bureau of Ships

89. Bureau of Ships, "An Administrative History of the Bureau of Ships during World War II." Washington. 1952. 1,218 pp., appendices.

A history of the administration of the Bureau of Ships from 1940 until early 1946 is provided in these four volumes. Following a brief discussion delineating the Bureau's origins, the first volume outlines the enlargement and reorganization of the Bureau to meet the impending crisis of world war. Particular attention is focused on efforts to recruit additional personnel and to expand federal and private shipbuilding facilities.

Volume II covers the post Pearl Harbor period through the beginning of 1943. The success of the Bureau's salvage efforts in Hawaii following the Japanese attack, as well as later salvage activities, are treated in detail. Continuing expansion of personnel and facilities is discussed along with the production and allocation of scarce materials.

In discussing the Bureau's operation from early 1943 until the victory over Japan, Volume III opens with an overview of naval strategy at the midpoint of the war and examines overall policies of the Bureau. A lengthy review of the maintenance and repair of ships, and the distribution of spare parts follows. The Bureau's relationships with private industry and the Bureau's own production accomplishments also are considered.

The final volume describes the postwar adjustment of the bureau, covering such topics as navy yard reorganization, ship construction cancellations, and personnel reductions. In addition, the wartime importance of research and development is summarized. The impact of the 1946 atomic bomb test (Operation Crossroads) and the subsequent effect of nuclear warfare on Bureau planning is the final subject treated in the narrative.

Together with numerous charts and tables found throughout the text, twelve appendices supplement the narrative. Among the appendices are histories of various sections of the Bureau. The remaining material consists of charts and tables concerning ship construction, yard expansion, item pricing, and ship losses.

Bureau of Supplies and Accounts

90. Bureau of Supplies and Accounts, "Accounting Group and Disbursing Division." Washington. 1945. 284 pp., appendices.

The volume is divided into four parts, the first of which details the wartime activities of the Accounting Group. This organization was charged with maintaining accounts of the Navy's finances and properties. Included in this section is a narrative description of lend-lease and the complete "Grady Report" which recommended means to improve the efficiency of the Accounting Group.

The second section provides a history, from the end of World War I to the last year of World War II, of the Disbursing Division, which was responsible for administering payment of the Navy's military, civilian, and contractor personnel.

Part III relates the activities of the Officers' Accounts Division, which serviced officer pay records, during both world wars and in the interwar period. The division's performance in relation to the greatly increased workload of World War II is of particular interest.

The final section contains a narrative summary of the wartime operation of the Field Branch Liaison Division, which was the representative in Washington for the bureau's disbursing field branch in Cleveland, Ohio.

The four parts contain charts, graphs, manuals, and correspondence, either appended to the narratives or integrated into them.

91.   Bureau of Supplies and Accounts, "Supplying the Aeronautical Establishment." Washington. 1945. 325 pp.

The wartime provision of logistic support to the Navy's air arm is thoroughly detailed in this narrative history. The development of aviation supply procedures and organization is traced from World War I and the interwar years through World War II. The Bureau of Supplies and Accounts' Aviation Supply Division and its successor, the Aviation Supply Liaison Division, operated in coordination with the Bureau of Aeronautics in the procurement, accounting, cataloging, and distribution of aviation material. The activities of the Aviation Supply Office in Philadelphia, manned jointly by the two bureaus, also are discussed.

Included in the narrative are numerous photographs, charts, tables, letters, and circulars. Extracts from such key documents as the Yarnell Report, a Booz, Fry, Allen, and Hamilton Report, and from materials relating to the Radford Board, all of which dealt with a reorganization of aviation supply administration, complement the text.

92.   Bureau of Supplies and Accounts, "History of the Clothing Division." Washington. 1945. 304 pp.

This volume concerning the organization charged with procurement, research and development, maintenance, and the provision of clothing for naval personnel, is divided into three chronological sections.

Part I details the activities of the Clothing Division from the time of its separation from the Subsistence and Clothing Division in 1940 to early 1944. Among the organization's duties were inspecting and testing fabrics, preparing uniform specifications, and maintaining records listing purchase prices and stocks on hand, requisitioning clothing for lend-lease, and determining Navy-wide requirements.

Parts II and III, covering a shorter period of time (June 1944 to March 1945), treat subjects found in the first part. Also discussed are such matters as the Mobile Display Unit which exhibited Navy Uniforms in order to motivate textile workers.

The narratives include price lists, organizational charts, issue lists, photographs, pertinent correspondence, uniform cataloges, clothing manuals, and contracts.

The author of the history was Marguerite A. Kearney.

93. Bureau of Supplies and Accounts, "Wartime History of the Cost Inspection Service." Washington. 1945. 189 pp., appendices.

The narrative section of this history comprises two parts. The first covers the period from World War I (when the Cost Inspection Service was established) to June 1944, while the second deals with the activities of the organization during July 1944 to December 1945. A third section consists of numerous appended documents. A thorough condensation of the history also is included.

Organized to oversee the determination of

shipbuilding and ship repair costs, the Cost Inspection Service handled such duties as negotiation, renegotiation, and termination of contracts; inspection of contractor cost estimates; development of standard accounting procedures; maintenance of current manuals, bulletins, and instructions; and the conduct of periodic audits.

Appendices include correspondence, sample contracts, working forms, instructions to contractors and inspectors, bureau publications, and manuals.

The author of the volume was Lieutenant Commander P. M. Mattisen, (SC) USNR.

94. Bureau of Supplies and Accounts, "History of the Fuel Division." Washington. 1945. 201 pp.

This volume contains a detailed description of the wartime activities of the Fuel Division. Following a brief background discussion of the organization's evolution from World War I, the narrative treats such topics as the policies and procedures involved in the determination of fuel requirements, procurement, specifications, and the transportation and storage of fuel stocks. Relationships with other services, government agencies, and with foreign governments, as well as the impact of the war on the domestic fuel industry, also are dealt with in the text. The Fuel Division handled diesel oil, aviation gasoline, motor gasoline, lubricating oils, and solid fuels.

The narrative is interspersed with relevant graphs, charts, and tables depicting the Navy's fuel supply system.

95.	Bureau of Supplies and Accounts, "History of the Stock Division." Washington. 1945. 410 pp., appendices.

This administrative history consists of two narrative volumes and one volume of exhibits. Essentially, the work is a compilation of separate histories for each of the division's branches. Topics covered include the wartime development of general policies, such as the decision to improve stock accounting and inventory control procedures through the use of tabulating machines, the promulgation of consolidated stock reports, and efforts to adapt old as well as innovative stock control systems to the massive wartime increase in supply items procured and stocked. Also dealt with are the several organizational changes undergone by the cataloguing branch during the war and the advent of the Navy Standard Stock Catalogue, precursor of the federal catalogue system.

Photographs of division work areas, pertinent correspondence, and stock control publications accompany the text.

The appendix volume contains various correspondence, supply catalogs, a listing of comments regarding the catalogues from organizations in the field, manuals, and planning material.

96.	Bureau of Supplies and Accounts, "History of the Maintenance Division." Washington. 1945. 115 pp., appendix.

The narrative history of the Maintenance Division, renamed the Budget Division in 1944, details the organizational evolution of the office from World War I to 1945. This administrative entity was eventually charged with budgetary cognizance over all bureau appropriations within the bureau.

The text is divided into four chronological parts that summarize the duties and accomplishments of the various internal sections. Among these subdivisions were the Standards Section, which advised field activities on the most efficient use of office equipment and supplies; and the Defense Aid Section, which oversaw budget control of lend-lease requisitions until the establishment of the International Aid Division in 1944.

A number of charts, tables, and orders are contained in the narrative.

Lieutenant John R. Talmage, SC(S), USNR, and Lieutenant (junior grade) Robert P. Williams, SC(S), USNR, were the authors of this history.

97. Bureau of Supplies and Accounts, "History--International Aid Division." Washington. 1946. 54 pp., appendices.

Formed in 1944, the International Aid Division combined the administrative and accounting functions related to lend-lease and other forms of foreign aid. The relatively brief narrative treats the activity of the division during most of 1944 and 1945. Two of the history's parts detail the work of the Administration Section and the Accounting and Statistical Section. The final part relates the history of the division as a whole in the last eleven months of the war.

In addition to discussing the supply of military equipment to Allied countries, the text covers such special topics as the development of a system of marking aid material to indicate its American origin, establishment of foreign disbursement centers, and transportation of foreign nationals within the United States. Appended documents, consisting of reports, conference minutes, and key correspondence, follow the last two sections of narrative.

Lieutenant John R. Talmage, SC(S), USNR, was the author of this history.

98. Bureau of Supplies and Accounts, "Packaging and Materials Handling." Washington. 1945. 87 pp.

This volume consists of a predominantly visual representation of the functions and procedures of the Field Operations Branch, General Stock Division. Photographs, flow charts, tables, and a map serve to illustrate the wartime methods of packaging materials for shipment overseas and of handling supplies during transshipment to the operating forces. Various aspects of these functions, such as strapping, weighing, and stenciling containers; corrosion prevention; packing and crating; proper fork-lift operation; cargo handling; and material palletization are depicted.

This pictorial summary is organized according to the organization of the branch. A brief narrative describing the mission of each subordinate entity and its accomplishments precedes the visual matter. A short history of the wartime organizational transformation of the Field Operations Branch from the Containers Division, Office of Procurement and Material, prefaces the overall work.

99. Bureau of Supplies and Accounts, "History of Officer Personnel Division" and "History of Chief Clerk's Division." Washington. 1945. 71 pp., appendices.

The Officer Personnel Division was responsible for the personnel administration of Supply Corps officers. The narrative description of the division's wartime activities discusses such functions as planning for future personnel requirements and the use of civilian sources of recruitment; maintaining a constant rate of trained male and female officers entering the logistic service; advising the Bureau of Naval Personnel on courses of instruction recommended for Supply Corps officers; and planning the rotation and assignment of personnel.

The exhibits include tables, board reports, and correspondence relating to the training and commissioning of Naval Reserve officers to support the logistic war effort.

The final section details the work from 1917 to 1945 of the Chief Clerk's Division, which was charged with administering the mail, files, messengers, space, office equipment, and maintenance personnel of the bureau. Several tables and an organizational chart are interspersed in the text.

100.   Bureau of Supplies and Accounts, "Supplying the Fleet." 2 vols. Washington. 1945. 479 pp.

This history, consisting of two separately bound volumes, is primarily a photographic synopsis of the wartime functioning of the Bureau of Supplies and Accounts headquarters in Washington. The study also provides a visual identification of key staff personnel, their work areas, and equipment utilized to expedite supply procedures. The text is divided in accordance with the bureau's organization. The duties and accomplishments of divisions and subordinate sections in the bureau are briefly summarized.

The author was Lieutenant Paul W. Bruske, SC(S), USNR.

101.   Bureau of Supplies and Accounts, "Administrative Planning Division," and "History of Advanced Base Section and the Logistic Planning Division (December 1942 - April 1945) -- Supplying the Advanced Bases." 4 vols. Washington. 1945. 227 pp., appendices.

The histories in this work emphasize the planning process involved in supplying the Fleet and overseas bases.

Parts I and II detail the many comprehensive organizational changes undergone by the bureau's various planning activities. These divisions, by their nature, were concerned with all facets of the logistic effort.

The Administrative Planning Division dealt with such matters as planning for the outfitting of ships, control of publications, bureau public relations, liaison with Congress, and supervision of the bureau's interests in military government. The division was charged also with compiling the wartime administrative history of the Bureau of Supplies and Accounts. The narrative provides valuable information regarding the inception and development of the historical project which was under the overall supervision of the Office of Naval History.

Part II contains an account of the bureau's logistics planning function during World War II, with a focus on the expansion and implementation of the advanced base concept. The text describes the procedures involved in establishing and supplying the numerous Pacific island bases.

Photographs of staff personnel and supply operations, as well as several officer rosters, accompany the narrative.

Appendices are included in the final section of the narrative volume and in three separate volumes. Bureau publications dealing with planning in general are appended to the text, while the second volume of the exhibits is divided between correspondence, handbooks, conference notes, and a newsletter, related either to the Administrative Planning or the Logistic Planning divisions. The third and fourth volumes contain organization charts, orders, correspondence, plans, manuals, guides, and photographs related to the administration of the Navy's military government program.

102.   Bureau of Supplies and Accounts, "First Draft of Administrative History of Supply Corps. Procurement in World War II (Interim Report)." Washington. 1945. 233 pp.

This comprehensive summary describes the development of Navy procurement policies and procedures from the early years of the nation through the end of World War II. The narrative treats such aspects as the purchase of clothing, rubber, lumber, food, and fuel. The fundamental wartime organizational changes experienced by the bureau's procurement activities also are detailed. The final section deals with the question of consolidating certain Army-Navy procurement functions.

The appendices are voluminous and contain relevant reports, correspondence, tables, plans, charts, sample stock catalogs, and the history of a field purchasing unit. Numerous photographs are located throughout both the text and the appendices.

The author was Lieutenant James E. Colvin, SC(S), USNR, who states that the work was based on the Purchase Division history for which Lieutenant Margaret Ocker, SC(W), USNR, was responsible.

103. Bureau of Supplies and Accounts, "A History of Purchasing within the Supply Group, World War II." Washington. 1945. 459 pp., appendices.

The narrative summarizes the wartime activities of the bureau's various purchasing sections. Special emphasis is given to the work of the Purchase Division, which had general oversight of the bureau's buying functions.

Structural transformations of purchasing organizations are described at length with pertinent documents interspersed in the text. The subject of purchasing is treated both topically and chronologically, although only the years 1944 and 1945 are covered in the latter manner. Such facets of this logistic task as purchasing raw materials and manufactured products; negotiating, renegotiating, and terminating contracts; and field purchasing are related.

Included within the narrative are several photographs of key personnel, correspondence, organizational charts, directives, and reports.

The appendices contain a listing of sources used in compiling the history and a roster of officers serving with the General Purchase Division in early 1944.

The author of this volume was Lieutenant Margaret Ocker, SC(W), USNR.

104. Bureau of Supplies and Accounts, "Historical Record of the Subsistance Division." Washington. 1945. 190 pp.

This history of the Subsistance Division provides a thorough description of the unit's various sections and their duties. Functions of the division included maintaining inventories and stock reports of the quantity and condition of provisions at distributing points, determining

Navy food requirements and procurement policies, awarding contracts, administering the delivery of subsistence items, supervising food inspections and tests, developing special rations, improving methods of food preparation, administering commissary stores, and handling the Navy food rationing system.

The narrative details the change from peacetime to wartime procurement methods and the division's dealings with other services and government agencies concerned with food supply, as well as the organization's growth during World War II.

Numerous photographs depicting various stages of food preparation and storage accompany the text, as do several charts, rosters, and lists of field operations.

105. Bureau of Supplies and Accounts, "Synopsis of Ship's Store Division Accomplishments, 1 June 1944 to 1 September 1945." Washington. 1945. 14 pp., appendices.

This summary of the Ship's Store Division's activities during World War II also relates to the supply of subsistence items. Established in July 1944, the division oversaw the operations of consolidated ship's stores and ship's service stores. The former had functioned as part of the Navy supply system, while the latter had operated under the Bureau of Naval Personnel and utilized unappropriated funds.

The brief narrative describes the division's achievements in increasing the efficiency in the operation and management of ship's stores during late 1944 and 1945. Accomplishments included the establishment of soft drink bottling plants, barber shops, and laundries in forward areas. Measures to increase shipments of such items as radios, record players, and magazines to the operating forces also are discussed.

The appendix section contains organizational charts, memoranda, reports, and conference notes dealing with the provision of supplies to ship's stores and their administration.

106.   Bureau of Supplies and Accounts, "History of the Storage Division." Washington. 1945. 105 pp., appendices.

The Storage Division resulted from the consolidation in March 1944 of the former Storage Section of the Stock Division, and the Research, Development and Storage Projects Section of the Planning Division. However, this history details the development of Navy storage and warehousing policies and procedures from the time of World War I. The subject matter is treated in fourteen narrative parts and an appendix section. In addition to treating these subjects from a bureau point of view, many naval supply depots are dealt with separately.

The account focuses on the great wartime expansion of facilities construction, space allocation procedures, warehousing techniques, storage site leasing, and the temperature and humidity control of stored goods. Accompanying the text are photographs of storage areas, tables indicating storage space available in depots at certain periods of time, and extracts from pertinent correspondence.

The greater part of this volume consists of appended orders, press clippings, cost estimates, plans, correspondence, reports, storage manuals, sample forms, bureau publications, directives, and committee statements.

107.   Bureau of Supplies and Accounts, "History of the Transportation Division." Washington. 1944. 72 pp., appendices.

Prior to 1943, the Transportation Division was known as the Traffic Section of the Fuel and Transportation Division. The history details the activities of this Navy function from 1919, through the interwar period, and into World War II.

Arranged topically, the narrative treats all the modes of transportation. It discusses such subjects as the wartime growth of the San Francisco area as a shipping center for the Pacific, the creation of the Naval Air Transportation Service, the establishment of District Property Transportation Offices, the consolidation of Army and Navy transcontinental rail shipments, and efforts to expedite the movement of Navy material.

The organization of the Transportation Division is described at length. Its various sections, including Defense Aid Material Movement, Ships and Advanced Base, Commerce, Motor Transport, and Household Effects, are covered in separate discussions.

The appendices consist of the comprehensive "Navy Traffic Flow Study, 1943-1944" and its supplement for January to July 1945, both of which contain statistical tables, charts, and maps. The "Navy Shipment Marking Handbook" also is appended to the text.

Bureau of Yards and Docks

108.   Bureau of Yards and Docks, <u>Building the Navy's Bases in World War II: History of the Bureau of Yards and Docks and the Civil Engineer Corps, 1940-1946</u> (Washington: GPO, 1947), 2 vols., 818 pp., index, appendix.

These two volumes recount the bureau's global endeavors in support of the Navy's war effort. The unpublished manuscript upon which this printed work was based has not been located. Arranged in three narrative parts, the published history provides a comprehensive description of the work of the bureau headquarters, the Civil Engineer Corps, and the Construction Battalions (Seabees).

In Part I, the topics covered include planning the public works program, financing wartime construction projects, the organizational development of the bureau and the Civil Engineer Corps, problems of construction contracting, logistic support for advanced bases, the establishment and growth of the Seabees, and the provision of advanced base equipment.

The second part concentrates on the construction of bases in the continental United States. The various facilities and installations are treated according to the nature of their primary function in sections describing navy yards and stationary drydocks, floating drydocks, air stations, training stations, supply depots, ammunition depots, and hospitals. Defense and emergency rental housing, civil works, and minor construction programs are subjects separately discussed.

Part III focuses on the establishment and construction of advanced bases, with each narrative section representing a geographic area. The text details the problems encountered in building advanced bases at such diverse locations as Adak, Alaska; the Galapagos Islands; Trinidad; Le Havre, France; Sardinia, and Okinawa and Iwo Jima in the Pacific. The construction of all types of buildings, wharfs, roadways, pipelines, fuel tanks, ship repair facilities, airfields, and power plants is related. The work of the Seabees in rehabilitating captured ports, operating beach camps, and in transporting, installing, and operating ferries, piers, and artificial harbors during the invasion of Europe is one of many topics of particular interest.

Graphs, organizational charts, maps, and numerous photographs of airfields, port installations, training facilities, warehouses, construction equipment, ships, and craft, bridges, barracks, ammunition storage areas, fuel farms, factories, drydocks, and other man-made structures, as well as personnel, are interspersed in the text.

An appendix section provides a list of Seabee units, with dates of commissioning and inactivation and places of overseas service indicated.

SHORE ESTABLISHMENT

Naval Districts

109.   Commandant First Naval District, "History of Naval Administration, World War II," Vols. I-XI (bound in 6 vols.). Boston. 1946. 2,292 pp., appendices.

The history of the First Naval District thoroughly details the administration of this command, which comprised most of the New England states. The eleven volumes in the history include many documents and photographs in addition to the basic narrative.

Volume I discusses the geographical character, industry, port facilities, and prewar naval shore establishment of New England, as well as the prewar and wartime lines of authority, responsibilities, composition, organizational development, and relationships with other services in the area.

In Volume II, various aspects of personnel administration are covered, including the major policy decisions made during 1939-1941, the years of total mobilization, and 1945 when the planned reductions in forces began. Individually treated are district staff sections, among them the Women's Reserve, chaplain, vocational training, discipline, welfare, labor relations, Selective Service, industrial manpower, civilian personnel, and safety engineering subdivisions.

Part I of the third volume relates the origins, composition, and structural evolution of the Naval Local Defense Force command; contains separate histories of subordinate section bases, harbor defense control posts, and naval frontier bases; and provides a compilation of Allied air and ship losses in district waters. The second part covers the activities of the Northern Group, Eastern Sea Frontier, particularly in sea-air rescue, harbor defense, shipping lane patrol, minesweeping, and air operations.

Volume IV recounts the wartime functioning of the District Operations, Logistics, Communications, Public Relations, Security, and Property Transportation Offices as well as that of the Port Director.

In Volume V, the first part discusses aspects of the District Supply Office's mission relating to war production and procurement, cost inspection, the War Savings Bond program, and the Navy Relief Society. Part II deals with public works activities throughout the district and in the Boston Navy Yard. Part III provides individual histories of district medical facilities and covers such special topics as the Cocoanut Grove disaster and venereal disease control.

The sixth volume treats the organizational evolution of the District Intelligence Office, its administrative workings, and the counterintelligence, plant protection, investigative, training, and coastal information collection facets of its operational mission.

Volume VII comprises a documentary supplement to the preceding volume.

Volume VIII provides a narrative description of the work done by district industrial establishments in support of the war effort. The naval shipyards at Boston and Portsmouth,

109. New Hampshire; the privately owned ship construction facilities at Bath, Maine and Quincy, Massachusetts; the Naval Ammunition Depot at Hingham, Massachusetts; and the Naval Torpedo Station at Newport, Rhode Island are discussed in detail.

Composed of 150 photographs, Volume IX provides visual representation of the wartime activities of the district industrial installations dealt with in the previous volume.

In Volume X, the text contains histories of the naval bases and stations at Argentia, Newfoundland; Portland, Maine; Newport, and Quonset, Rhode Island, in addition to the Naval Net Depot at Newport and the Civil Engineer Corps Officer Training School at Davisville, Rhode Island. A pictorial section complements the work.

The final volume concentrates on the various district training programs and facilities. The narrative describes the administration of the V-12 Program (designed to provide qualified officer candidates with an advanced educational background) and the conduct of training in communications, radar, local defense, and fire fighting at naval schools. The programs at the Maine and Massachusetts maritime academies and the Women's Reserve school at Smith College also are explored.

Extensive documentary material is either integrated within the text or appended in separate volumes. It consists of maps, tables, charts, diagrams, organizational and adminstrative manuals, flow charts, pertinent letters, memoranda, basic directives, rosters, and photographs of airfields, facilities, personnel, and ships.

This comprehensive work was prepared under the direction of Captain James A. Lewis, USNR.

110. Commandant Third Naval District, "Historical Summary of the Third Naval District." 5 vols. New York. 1946. 681 pp., appendices.

Following a brief summary of the history of the Third Naval District staff and its wartime activities, the volumes in this series separately treat the district command and the various subordinate functions located throughout New York, Connecticut, and northern New Jersey.

In volume one, the narrative details the workings of the offices of the Commandant, his Chief of Staff, and the Assistant Commandant (Operations), as well as the District Planning and Coordinating Office. Topics covered include the development of the organizational structure, relationships with other Navy commands and other services, personnel matters, reductions in the shore establishment at the end of the war, and the decommissioning of ships and berthing sites.

Volume two consists of individual narrative histories of the Port Director, New York; the Harbor Entrance Control Post, New York Harbor; and the district's Naval Armed Guard Center. In Part I, the sections of the Port Director's staff dealing with merchant ship procurement, operations, routing and convoys, harbor movements, armed guards, logistics, and administration are covered. The second part details many facets of the naval armed guard program, in particular training, manpower problems, funding, supply support, personnel administration, and operational achievements. The final section describes the physical characteristics of New York harbor, war plans and defense measures, interservice cooperation, wartime expansion of port facilities, personnel and training problems, and communication and radar procedures as they relate to the Harbor Entrance Control Post command. Also discussed are the activities of subordinate units located throughout the New York City area and in New Jersey.

The three volumes of appendix material contain flow charts, rosters, reports, manuals,

minutes of meetings, letters, operation plans
and orders, pamphlets, hydrographic charts, composition of forces lists, bulletins, photographs,
and a narrative history of the Third Naval
District during World War I.

111. Commandant Fourth Naval District, "The War
History of the Fourth Naval District from Dec.
7th 1941." Vols. I-VI. Philadelphia,
Pennsylvania. 1946. approx. 1,500 pp.

  Comprising sixteen narrative parts, this
voluminous account details the wartime admini=
strative and operational functioning of the
Fourth Naval District. The district's headquarters was in Philadelphia and its area of
responsibility was Pennsylvania, Delaware, and
Southern New Jersey.

  The first part provides a description of
local geography, the naval shore establishment,
and the district's prewar history. This is
followed by a brief discussion of the headquarters
staff and its growth. Part III is further
divided into two sections, the first of which
covers working relationships within the district
command, with other Navy commands, and with
other services. Task Group 02.4 (Delaware Group),
Eastern Sea Frontier, is the subject of the
second subdivision, with emphasis on the conduct
of operations by this local defense force.

  A detailed history of the Philadelphia Navy
Yard comprises Part IV. The narrative traces
the development of the installation from 1798 to
1945, but the greatest emphasis is placed on
the administration of the navy yard and its shipbuilding and industrial contributions during the
war.

  Part V consists of a brief summary of the
District Supply Office's personnel composition,
organizational evolution, and responsibilities.

Parts VI, VII, and VIII explore the many aspects of naval aviation in the Fourth Naval District. In addition to a brief history of the naval air bases command, which controlled the Naval Air Facility at New Cumberland, Pennsylvania, and the Naval Air Stations at Cape May, Wildwood, and Atlantic City, New Jersey, and at Willow Grove, Pennsylvania, the narrative treats the work of the Naval Air Material Center at Philadelphia. The district's lighter-than-air program and Naval Air Station, Lakehurst, New Jersey, also are discussed.

Seven of the remaining eight parts provide topical coverage of various administrative functions--public works, procurement and personnel, training, medical affairs, communications, public relations, and postwar demobilization. Part XIV, a brief history of the Naval Ammunition Depot, Fort Mifflin, Pennsylvania, is filed separately.

Documentary material, consisting of maps, flow charts, correspondence, tables, graphs, blueprints, reports, and numerous photographs of personnel, ships and craft, airfields, naval bases, and other installations, is interspersed in the text.

The authors of this work, who are identified in the text, include Captain Dennis L. Francis, USN; Commanders Gardiner Luce (CEC), USNR, and Donald R. Keller (MC), USNR; Lieutenant Commander Solomon E. Zubrow, USNR; Lieutenants Myron D. Hockenbury (SC), USNR, John J. Kelley, USNR, and Kent S. Ehrman (CEC), USNR; Lieutenants (junior grade) Clifton E. Landwehr, USNR and Charlotte V. Lord (W), USNR; and Ensign Nettie T. Brown (W), USNR.

112.   Commandant Fifth Naval District, "History of the Fifth Naval District, 1939-1945." 7 vols. Norfolk, Virginia. 1946. 751 pp., appendices.

The Fifth Naval District was headquartered in Norfolk, Virginia, and was responsible for numerous naval facilities in the Chesapeake Bay region, the states of Virginia, Maryland, and West Virginia, and the northern coastal region of North Carolina. The basic history of the district (contained in volumes one and two) concentrates on administrative problems and achievements from the perspective of the commandant. Materials in five additional appendix volumes supplement the narrative by providing details on component offices in the district headquarters and some major subordinate commands.

The first three parts of the narrative describe the geographic features of the Fifth Naval District, its activities from 1903 to 1939, and the command's preparations for war in the 1939-1941 period of national emergency. In Part IV, the commandant's basic responsibilities as commander of the Fifth Naval District, the Naval Operating Base, Norfolk, and of the naval local defense forces are outlined, followed by a lengthy discussion of the organization and activities of his staff. That part concludes with a discussion on the World War II impact of the Navy on the Williamsburg, Virginia, area.

In the second volume, the narrative turns to a discussion of logistics and the operations of naval local defense forces. Among the logistical aspects discussed are personnel, supplies, transportation, and repair and maintenance activities. Operational subjects include harbor security, coastal minesweeping, and the protection of coastal shipping against German submarines.

The five appendix volumes present individual historical narratives and key documents relating to each of the major staff components of the Fifth Naval District Headquarters, ranging from the Assistant Chief of Staff for Personnel to the Domestic Transportation Officer. Among the documents are basic manuals and plans of the Fifth Naval District, minutes of staff conferences, and a brief history of the district during World War I. Histories are included for the following subordinate commands:

> Naval Operating Base, Norfolk
> Port Director, Fifth Naval District
> Senior Naval Officer Present (Ashore), Baltimore
> Assistant District Security Officer, Baltimore
> Harbor Entrance Control Post, Fort Story, Virginia
> Naval Training Station, NOB, Norfolk
> Naval Training Center, Bainbridge, Maryland
> Naval Training and Distribution Center, Camp Peary, Virginia
> Supervisor of Shipbuilding, Newport News, Virginia

The District Historical Officer during most of the period that this history was being written and compiled was Commander Christopher A. Russell, USNR.

113. Commandant Sixth Naval District, "History of the Sixth Naval District." 2 vols. Charleston, South Carolina. 1945. 604 pp., appendices.

This comprehensive and well organized account is divided into two narrative sections and an appendix section.

Part I provides a description of the geographical features, major seaports, shipping characteristics, major naval shore installations, and principal industrial plants within the boundaries of the Sixth Naval District (which included the states of North and South Carolina, Georgia, and Northern Florida), as well as a general summary of the district's history. The following material deals with the functioning of the district headquarters, focusing on the duties, growth, and coordination with other entities of the staff. Also covered are relationships between the district command and the Eastern Sea Frontier, Charleston Navy Yard, and Army commands. The final chapter treats such aspects of the operational mission as coastal patrol, net and boom defense, mine warfare, beach patrol, air-sea rescue, and antisubmarine warfare. This part is extensively footnoted.

In Part II, the text relates individually the work of the district administrative, logistics, and operations offices; the Joint Operations Center; the Port Director's Office; the Combat and Operational Intelligence Branch; the office of the Director of Women's Reserve; and the Navy and Marine facilities in Charleston, Parris Island, and Columbia, South Carolina; Asheville, Raleigh, and Chapel Hill, North Carolina; and Savannah, Georgia.

The text contains maps, graphs, flow charts, tables, rosters, and photographs of ships, facilities, and personnel.

The appended documents include histories of district operations during World War I, pertinent letters, memoranda, organization charts, orders, manuals, and diagrams.

Lieutenant Edward A. Hummel, USNR, authored this work.

114. Commandant Seventh Naval District, "Administrative History of the Seventh Naval District, 1 February 1942 - 14 August 1945." Miami, Florida. 1946. 103 pp., appendices.

The rather brief history of the Seventh Naval District (which comprised most of Florida) provides a description of the district's geographical and climatological characteristics and of the major naval shore installations established within the command area. The evolution of the district command is traced from the early years of the century through mid-1942, when the organizational structure under which the district operated for the remainder of the war was established. Relationships with the Gulf Sea Frontier and the Sixth Naval District are emphasized. The administrative activities of the headquarters are discussed at some length, with each subordinate staff function receiving individual treatment. Following an overall description of the headquarters, the workings of the Commandant's Office; the Assistant Chiefs of Staff for operations, administration, logistics, and personnel; and the district public works, medical, intelligence, communications, public information, supply, and civilian personnel offices are detailed. The final chapter contains a list of district shore activities on March 1942, September 1942, and October 1945.

Throughout the text and in the appendices are located rosters, organizational charts, graphs, maps, tables, hydrographic charts, letters, orders, messages, and an organization manual dated September 1943.

The author of the narrative was Lieutenant Francis X. McCarthy, USNR.

115. Commandant Eighth Naval District, "History of the Eighth Naval District." New Orleans, Louisiana. 1946. 339 pp., appendices.

Following several introductory chapters, this history of the largest naval district in the Gulf States area is arranged according to the Command's organizational structure. The functions of subordinate commands and offices are explored separately and in detail.

The initial section deals with the physical and economic characteristics of the district and its naval shore establishment, which consisted of repair bases, advanced base depots, ordnance plants, ammunition depots, and training facilities. The second section briefly traces the historical development of the command from the early years of the century to the end of World War II. Chapters Three, Four, and Five treat the organizational evolution and wartime functioning of the headquarters staff and the command's relationships with other services and naval forces.

The remaining chapters cover the work of the various administrative offices in the headquarters, including those concerned with intelligence, communications, war plans, logistics, public information, the Women's Reserve, war bonds, and black personnel. The activities of the district Port Director, the Industrial Manager, and Commander Naval Air Bases also are discussed.

Located in the appendix section, and in several instances in the text, are tables, historical summaries, site plans, hydrographic charts, maps, a list identifying pertinent correspondence, organizational charts, composition of forces tables, a listing of all past commandants and wartime office heads, and graphs.

116.   Commandant Ninth Naval District, "Administrative History." 3 vols. Great Lakes, Illinois. 1946. 936 pp., appendices.

This work details the wartime administration of the Ninth Naval District, which included thirteen North Central and Mid-Western states. The account is divided into two parts. The first contains a general discussion of the command, while the second part treats individually the district's subordinate offices and functions.

An appendix volume complements the narrative.

Part I comprises a description of the geographical nature of the naval district's operational area and its industrial capacity. It also provides a summary of the district's history from the years prior to World War I through 1945. Command relations between the commandant and the district shore activities are explored, with emphasis on the findings of the Manpower Survey Committee, the Committee for Standardization of Terminology for Activities of the Navy, and the Committee to Study Command Relationships in Naval Districts (Farber Committee).

In Part II, the work of each administrative subdivision within the command is treated, including the medical, public works, supply, ordnance, operations, communications, domestic transportation, security, intelligence, and legal offices, as well as the Port Director, the Director of Naval Reserve, and the Director of Women's Reserve.

The appendix contains several photographs, organization charts, committee reports, pertinent letters, staffing records, site plans, graphs, circulars, statistical tables, instructions, manuals, and bulletins.

117.   Commandant Tenth Naval District, "Administrative Narrative." San Juan, Puerto Rico. 1946. 107 pp.

This relatively brief account opens with a description of the district's boundaries in the Caribbean area and a discussion of the command's history prior to America's entry into World War II. The balance of the account primarily details the activities of naval air and surface forces operating within the naval district's area of responsibility.

118.   Commandant Eleventh Naval District, "Administrative History." San Diego, California. 1946. 614 pp.

   Headquartered in San Diego, the Eleventh Naval District comprised Southern California; Clark County, Nevada; and the states of Arizona and New Mexico. This account consists of four narrative parts discussing separate topics.

   Part I relates the early history of the district and the development of the command and staff stucture. Each of the subordinate administrative offices is described separately in discussions of planning, air and sea operations, personnel, transportation control, and other functions of the staff. Relationships with the Western Sea Frontier also are treated.

   In the second part, the text treats the problems involved in establishing and expanding ammunition and ordnance facilities within the district. Development of the installations at Fallbrook, Seal Beach, the Camp Pendleton Boat Basin, San Diego Bay, and the Naval Ordnance Test Station at Inyokern is covered, with emphasis on site planning and selection, land acquisition, construction, and labor relations.

   In Part III, the narrative details many facets of district air activities, including the functioning of the Naval Air Station, San Diego; the utilization of auxiliary naval air stations throughout Southern California; the lighter-than-air program; the operation of Marine air stations at Santa Barbara, El Centro, Mojave, El Toro, and Miramar; and the administration of the aeronautical establishment.

   The final part treats several aspects of personnel relations, such as civilian recruitment, the Selective Service System, deferments, vocational training, dependent housing, and the activities of the Women's Reserve in support of the war effort.

   Following each chapter is a listing of

sources used.

The author of this work was Lieutenant Charles C. Cumberland, USNR.

119. Commandant Twelfth Naval District, "Administrative History, Twelfth Naval District, 1939-1945." 4 vols., San Francisco, California. 1946. 2,318 pp., appendices.

This voluminous account traces the activities of the naval district headquartered in San Francisco, whose area of responsibility included northern California and Nevada and the entire states of Utah and Colorado. In addition to documenting the activities of the commandant's office, the volumes include detailed information on a number of subordinate commands and offices.

Part I of the narrative discusses the district in 1939 and the preparedness steps taken prior to American entry into World War II. A general description of the headquarters staff and its reorganization during the war years is contained in the second part. The work of individual staff units (including naval and civilian personnel, womens reserve, legal, medical, Marine office, security, intelligence-public information, local defense forces, communications, planning, public works, domestic transportation, operations, ammunition and ordnance, aviation, supply office, property transportation, and office of the port director) is covered at length in Part III. The final part of the narrative is a relatively brief assessment of command relationships with other commands and offices, physically located within the district, but outside the district organization.

A volume of appendices includes separate histories of the following subordinate commands:

    U. S. Naval Training and Distribution Center, Treasure Island

U. S. Naval Section Base, U. S.
  Naval Frontier Base, San Francisco
Yerba Buena Island (Receiving Ship),
  San Francisco
U. S. Navy Chemical Warfare Training
  Unit, Dugway Proving Ground, Utah
Camp Parks, Shoemaker, California
U. S. Naval Disciplinary Barracks,
  Shoemaker, California
U. S. Naval Barracks (Embarkation),
  Treasure Island

The Historical Section of the Twelfth Naval District, which compiled this history, was headed successively by Lieutenant Commander C. E. Odegaard, USNR, and Lieutenant Commander John W. Collins, USNR.

120.   Commandant Thirteenth Naval District, "Administrative History of the Thirteenth Naval District." 4 vols. Seattle, Washington. 1946. 1,723 pp., appendices.

The Thirteenth Naval District was headquartered in Seattle, Washington, and included the states of Washington, Oregon, Montana, Idaho, and Wyoming. Prior to April 1944, Alaska also was part of this district. Throughout most of World War II, the Commandant of the Thirteenth Naval District additionally commanded the Northwest Sea Frontier.

The first volume of this work traces the district's historical background prior to America's entry into World War II with emphasis on preparations for war during 1939-1941 and the situation as of December 1941. A discussion follows of the commandant's responsibilities (especially in his capacity as Commander Northwest Sea Frontier) for assigned surface and air forces that had the primary task of protecting coastal shipping in the Northwest Pacific.

Volume two describes in great detail the administrative aspects of the sea frontier's operational forces, including their organization, bases, intelligence support, and the doctrine established for specific types of warfare. Following a discussion of logistics, this volume concludes by summarizing joint operations in the Thirteenth Naval District with Army, Canadian, and Soviet forces. The district's contact with the Soviets was primarily for the purpose of supporting their merchant shipping transporting supplies from Alaska and the Pacific Northwest.

The history's third volume concentrates on the administration of specific components in the district's headquarters. The areas covered in particular detail include public works, shipbuilding and repair, supplies and accounts, and civilian personnel. This section is followed by a thorough discussion of the relationships of the Thirteenth Naval District with both senior and subordinate commands that had interests in the Pacific Northwest.

Numerous documents are included within the basic text of this history. A number of additional letters, organization charts, messages, plans, and similar materials are bound as volume four. These records are arranged by the specific chapters of the text to which they relate.

121. Commandant Fourteenth Naval District, "Administrative History of the Fourteenth Naval District and the Hawaiian Sea Frontier." 5 vols. Pearl Harbor, Hawaii. 1945. 803 pp., appendices.

Following a discussion of the extensive geographic area covered by the Fourteenth Naval District (the Hawaiian archipelago, including Midway; the Palmyra, Johnson, and Washington atolls; and adjacent sea areas), this account discusses the evolution of American interest in the area, the development of Pearl Harbor as a naval base, and the general history of the Navy in the region through the end of World War II.

Subsequent chapters in the two-volume narrative section of the history trace the World War II experiences of separate components of the naval district staff. These included offices handling naval and civilian personnel, transportation, communications, medical and dental affairs, intelligence, cable and radio censorship, security, public information, supply, public works, logistics, material and ordnance, ships, service, legal matters, training, recreation and morale, British naval liaison, benefits and insurance, hydrographic matters, and Navy Relief. The narrative concludes with four topical chapters. One addresses the activities of the port director of the Naval Transportation Service who was responsible for the convoy and routing of merchant shipping in the area and related duties. It is followed by discussions of fishery rights in the naval district and the composition and functions of naval local defense forces that were assigned to the district. The final chapter assesses the commandant's role as Commander of the Hawaiian Sea Frontier. In this capacity, he commanded sea and ground forces responsible for the defense of the island of Oahu.

A large group of basic source documents, arranged according to the chapter that they support, appears in three appendix volumes. These include correspondence, memoranda, photographs, statistical tables, manuals, organization charts, plans, and similar materials.

The head of the district historical section, during the period that these volumes were being prepared, was Lieutenant James F. Collins, USNR.

122.   Commandant Fifteenth Naval District, "Administrative History, Fifteenth Naval District and Panama Sea Frontier." Balboa, Canal Zone. 1947. Vols. I-II. 474 pp., appendices.

    The Commandant of the Fifteenth District controlled naval activities in the Panama Canal Zone. In his additional capacity as Commander of the Panama Sea Frontier, he was responsible for the defense of the Pacific and Atlantic sea approaches to the canal and for naval shore facilities in the Central America region. The district and sea frontier headquarters were located in Balboa.

    The first volume of the history briefly treats the prewar and World War II organization of the command before turning to separate discussions of the district's staff offices. Some of the organizations covered include communications, education, Navy Weather Central, port director, provost marshal, and shore patrol. Volume I concludes with an account of the Panama Sea Frontier, including its organizational evolution, command relationships with the Army, and scope of operations. The district's organization manual is included as an annex. Other supplementary materials, including geographic and organizational charts, are inserted at appropriate places in the text.

    Volume II presents information on bases in the command area. A lengthy section discusses the Naval Operating Base, Balboa, which was composed of a number of subordinate shore commands. Despite its title, some of these activities were located at Coco Solo, Taboguilla Island, and Taboga Island. Additional chapters cover the Naval Operating Base, Coco Solo; Naval Radio Stations in Farfan, Gatun, and Summit; and the U. S. Naval Base, Puerto Castilla, Honduras. An appendix section is comprised of maps and photographs of several naval aviation facilities in Central America. Other photographs and charts are included in the basic text.

    The District Historical Officers during the

period that these volumes were being prepared were Lieutenant Leo J. Roland, USNR; Lieutenant (junior grade) John W. Buddeke, USNR; and Lieutenant Commander J. Clovis Smith, USNR.

Chief of Naval Operations Shore Activities

123. Office of the Chief of Naval Operations, "Hydrographic Office." Washington. n.d. 326 pp., appendix.

The mission of the Hydrographic Office was to collect, digest, and issue timely information contributing to the navigational safety of ships and aircraft at sea. The office produced and distributed various publication, such as charts, hydrographic bulletins, and sailing directions. To obtain information necessary for the publications, the organization undertook extensive research and maintained contact with other hydrographic organizations throughout the world.

The history focuses on the impact of World War II on the administration of the office. Following an initial explanation of the policies and responsibilities of the office, the narrative gives a detailed description of the wartime organization and the functions of its several divisions. A brief summary of the office's relations with other governmental agencies is presented. The remainder of the volume provides a year-by-year history of the changes and developments within the office from 1939 to 1945.

Appendices include numerous footnotes to the text and statistical compilations of items such as appropriations, personnel, and production during the 1938-1944 period.

124.   Office of the Chief of Naval Operations, "U. S. Naval Observatory." Washington. 1948. 119 pp., appendices.

Although submitted as part of the World War II administrative history project, this volume is a general history of the Naval Observatory. The first chapter describes the founding of the facility in 1842 and successive chapters trace the activity's contributions to astronomy and navigation. The Observatory's publications and the navigational and aerological instruments that it tested and produced are noted. A separate chapter details the development of the Observatory's Time Service, which provides the standard time for American navigators and others requiring accurate time. A chronology of events from 1809 to 1945, a list of superintendents, a summary of laws pertaining to the facility, and a history of the Observatory's library appear in other chapters.

Over half of the volume consists of appendices. These include numerous letters relating to the management of the observatory and a group of photographs showing various buildings and equipment. The author of the history was Commodore J. F. Hellweg, USN, Superintendent of the Observatory from 1930 to 1946.

125.   Office of the Chief of Naval Operations, "School of Oriental Languages." Washington. n.d. 36 pp., appendices.

Shortly before the outbreak of World War II, the Office of Naval Intelligence, recognizing the acute shortage of Japanese linguists, moved to establish courses in that language. In October 1941, instruction for naval students was begun at Harvard University and the University of California at Berkeley. The following June, all naval training in the language was centralized at the Navy Japanese Language School located on the campus of the University of Colorado. The administration of this school is the main focus of the brief narrative section of the volume. Besides outlining the organizational structure of the school, the text summarizes the instructional methods and the type of teaching materials employed. A few final remarks concern the addition in 1944 of other languages to the curriculum, including Chinese, Malay, and Russian. At that time the school was renamed the Navy School of Oriental Languages.

Numerous documents related to the administration of the school comprise the appendices. Many of these letters and reports are referred to specifically in the text. Several photographs and miscellaneous items, such as newspaper articles and graduation programs, also are found in this section.

126. Office of the Deputy Chief of Naval Operations (Air), "Naval Air Test Center, Patuxent River, Maryland." Vol. XII. Washington. 1945. 415 pp., appendices.

A history of the U. S. Naval Air Station, Patuxent River, Maryland is presented in this volume. That facility, which served as the Navy's flight-test center during World War II, was renamed the Naval Air Test Center in 1945.

The narrative is divided into three parts. Part I begins with a chronology of important events related to the air station from 1939 to 1945. A general discussion of the establishment of the base and its subsequent history to June 1945 follows. The second part outlines the organization, functions, and history of the air station's six test divisions (flight, electronics, armament, tactical, service, and test facilities). Part III is a history of the stations' numerous departments such as supply, public works, operations, and personnel.

Several of the six appendices contain documentary material, maps, and a list of buildings and other facilities. Other appendices include items related to various conferences and demonstrations held during the war, a summary of the early history of the station site and vicinity, and a list of officers and men who were killed on duty while attached to the air station. An extensive photographic section also is located in the appendices. Lieutenant Mary Louise Ford, USNR, was the editor of this history.

Bureau and Other Shore Activities

127.   Bureau of Ordnance, "Selected Ammunition Depots." 2 vols. Washington. n.d. 948 pp., appendices.

This work presents a series of brief histories of the wartime administration of several ammunition depots. Among the responsibilities of these facilities were assembly, storage, and shipment of ammunition and other ordnance equipment. Ammunition depots at Crane, Indiana; Fall Brook, California; Hingham, Massachusetts; and Hawthorne, Nevada are discussed in Volume I. A similar review of depots at McAlister, Oklahoma and St. Juliens Creek, Virginia appears in Volume II. Also covered in the second volume are the ordnance plants at Shumaker, Arkansas and Charlotte, North Carolina, as well as the naval magazine at Port Chicago, California.

The primary focus of most of the histories is on the organization and activities of the various facilities. The prewar history of certain depots is noted in the introduction to several of the narratives. Special topics, such as production problems and race relations, are elaborated upon in some cases. Several of the sections include appendices of charts and photographs.

128. Bureau of Ordnance, "Ordnance Plants." 2 vols. Washington. n.d. 702 pp., appendices.

The first volume of this set focuses on the Naval Ordnance Plant at Indianapolis, Indiana. Occupying about half the volume, the narrative details the construction and operation of the plant, which produced bombsights and fire-control equipment during World War II. Key sections of the discussion deal with personnel matters, training programs, and operational problems. The first of two lengthy appendices consists of sixteen source documents. Among these are organizational charts and diagrams of the plant structure. The second appendix contains photographs.

Brief histories of several other ordnance plants are provided in the second volume. The plants and type of operations discussed in each history are:

   a. Canton, Ohio: supplemental work from the Naval Gun Factory, Washington.

   b. Centerline, Michigan: work from the Naval Gun Factory, Washington, and parts for 20-millimeter guns.

   c. Forest Park, Illinois: production of torpedoes, particularly for aircraft.

   d. Pocatello, Idaho: manufacture, repair, and testing of various types of naval guns.

  e. South Charleston, West Virginia: production of gun barrels, torpedo air flasks, rocket parts, and related items.

  f. York, Pennsylvania: manufacture of 40-millimeter guns.

  Numerous charts, diagrams, and photographs, as well as a few key documents, accompany most of the histories.

129. Bureau of Ordnance, "U. S. Naval Gun Factory." Washington. 1945. 452 pp.

  Although the major emphasis of this work is on the wartime administration of the Washington Navy Yard and its associated activities, the first three chapters provide a general history of the facility from its beginning in 1799 through 1939. During most of its early history, the primary responsibility of the navy yard was the construction and maintenance of ships. However, by the 1880s, when the U. S. Naval Gun Factory was established in the yard, it had become an important center for ordnance production. On 1 December 1945, the overall activity was officially redesignated the Naval Gun Factory.

  Following the introductory chapters, the subsequent sections of the volume focus on the functions and activities of the many divisions and commands within the navy yard during the World War II era. The accounting, supply, medical, public works, and various production departments are among the activities that are covered. Also detailed is the work of the Experimental Model Basin, which was located at the yard until 1940, and of the Naval Photographic Intelligence Center. In addition, the wartime operation of a number of schools located at the yard is reviewed. Among these were schools providing training in ordnance and gunnery, deep-sea diving, mine disposal, electrical interior communications, and music.

A list of commandants of the navy yard and the Potomac River Command precede the narrative. Several photographs and maps are included in the text.

130.		Bureau of Ordnance, "Naval Torpedo Station, Newport, Rhode Island." Vols. I-VII (bound in 3 vols.). Washington. 1946. 922 pp., appendices.

This history provides a detailed examination of the history of the Naval Torpedo Station at Newport. The first volume is a chronology of important events associated with the station's history from its establishment in 1869 through 1945. Most of this material apparently was taken from earlier histories prepared in 1920 and 1939. A lengthy appendix of maps and photographs follows the chronology.

The subsequent three volumes focus on World War II. The first consists of the administration and organization manual used at the facility during the war. The other two are administrative histories of the same period, the first of which deals with major functions such as material procurement, design, and production. The second covers the operation of various service departments, including those responsible for supply, personnel, maintenance, medicine, and intelligence. A number of photographs, as well as organizational and production charts, are located in the text of the two histories.

Volume V is a collection of key documents cited in the footnotes to Volumes III, IV, VI, and VII. The station's role in the development of naval torpedoes from 1869 to the close of World War II is discussed in Volume VI. In addition, accounts of the overall evolution of torpedoes and examples of their operational employment in war are presented. Various photographs and diagrams of historic significance are found throughout the narrative. A selected bibliography and statistical appendices conclude the volume.

The seventh volume furnishes brief histories of the development of the Navy's electrical, chemical, and aircraft torpedoes. A similar treatment of exploder devices follows. Analysis is made of the merits, defects, and difficulties of the research and development related to each of these ordnance items. Several photographs supplement the text. An extract from a report on the torpedo experimental station at Eckernforde, Germany, and a chart comparing money spent on U. S. production and research projects are appended to the volume.

Clippings from various newspapers and periodicals, as well as a number of congressional documents, appear in the final volume of the set.

The author and compiler of the entire series was Robert J. H. Powel. A list of persons interviewed during the preparation of the volumes is attached to a letter of transmittal that also serves as the author's preface to the set.

131.   Bureau of Ordnance, "The History of the Naval Ordnance Laboratory, 1918-1945." 3 vols. Washington. 1946. 570 pp., appendices.

This series focuses on the history of the Naval Ordnance Laboratory, that originally was established in 1918 as the Bureau of Ordnance's Mine Laboratory. The first part is an administrative history of the facility from its founding to 1945. An introductory chapter provides information on the laboratory's early history, but the major emphasis of the subsequent chapters is on the organization and operation of its various offices and divisions during World War II. The final chapter deals with certain wartime problems that confronted the laboratory. Footnotes to the text, as well as a group of organizational charts, are included in the appendix.

Part II is a brief summary of the training program operated by the Ordnance Laboratory during the war. Among the enclosures that follow this discussion are a number of schedules and outlines of certain training courses.

The final part of the series provides a history of research and development programs undertaken by the laboratory. The two opening chapters of the narrative trace scientific activities related to mines and ammunition from 1919 to 1939. The remaining discussion concentrates on wartime programs, which primarily involved such underwater ordnance as mines, depth charges, and mine countermeasure gear. Also discussed is the development of other devices, including fuzes, flares, primers, and detonators, as well as specialized equipment used in the facility's work.

132.   Bureau of Ordnance, "Miscellaneous Activities." 2 vols. Washington. n.d. 929 pp., appendices.

The first section of this history focuses on the Naval Mine Warfare Test Station at Solomons, Maryland. After a brief review of the prewar origins of the installation, several subsequent chapters detail the functioning of its various departments during the war. The most important of these were the weapons department, which was responsible for testing underwater ordnance, and the countermeasures department. A final chapter is devoted to wartime accomplishments of the facility and recommendations for the future. Statistical tables, project lists, and organizational charts, as well as a large group of photographs, are located among the appendices to the work.

The other history in the first volume discusses the Naval Proving Ground at Dahlgren, Virginia. In reviewing the work of the installation since 1918, the narrative presents a comprehensive history of each division. Major emphasis is placed on functions during World War II. A number of photographs and organizational charts are found throughout the text.

Five shorter histories are located in the second volume. The first of these deals with the Naval Powder Factory at Indian Head, Maryland. Although only seventy-two pages in length, the study covers many important topics related to the operation of the factory during World War II. Among these are production, personnel, security, and wartime problems. Several graphs and photographs constitute the appendix. Similar coverage is provided in the second and third histories on the Naval Mine Depot at Yorktown, Virginia, and the Naval Ordnance Test Station at Inyokern, California. The former facility engaged in the manufacture of a considerable variety of mines, while the latter was responsible for developing and testing aircraft rockets. An appendix containing various maps, diagrams, and tables is included with the Yorktown history, while the Inyokern study is illustrated with many photographs.

The fourth section of the volume is a brief report on the Bureau of Ordnance Design Unit at Pasadena, California, that prepared production drawings, specifications, and instructions for items related to rocket research. The unit also coordinated various research and development efforts undertaken by the Inyokern Ordnance Test Station and the California Institute of Technology.

The last history examines the operation of the Naval Net Depot at Tiburon, California. Besides engaging in the production of nets, this installation had cognizance over net defenses for San Francisco Harbor. The administration of the net training and diving schools at the depot also is covered, as are the activities of the Shakedown Group that conducted training for ships assigned to laying nets. Numerous training, precommissioning, and shakedown schedules are among the appendices.

133. Bureau of Supplies and Accounts, "U. S. Naval Supply Depot, Oakland, California as of 31 December 1944." Washington. 1944. 223 pp.

This history treats the logistic activities of the Naval Supply Depot, Oakland, which was chosen because of its size and importance to represent the work of other naval supply depots during World War II. The narrative traces the growth of the depot from 1910, when serious consideration was given to its establishment, to the end of 1944, by which time the facility was operating at wartime efficiency.

The detailed account covers such aspects of the depot's functions as the reception, storage, issuance, transportation, and loading of all types of supply items destined for the operating forces in the Pacific. Special emphasis is given to the handling of fuel, aviation parts, advanced base components, and lend-lease material. The work of separate but subordinate organizations, such as the Navy Fuel Depot, Point Molate; the Navy Supply Sub-Depot, Stockton; and the Aviation Supply Annex, Oakland also is covered. Particular attention is devoted to the problems encountered in dealing with the dramatic increase of civilian employees during the war years.

Intermingled with the text are numerous photographs of the facilities, organization charts, rosters, tables, and correspondence.

134.	Naval Research Laboratory, "War History of the Naval Research Laboratory." Washington. 1946. 274 pp., appendices.

Although this history concentrates on the work of the Naval Research Laboratory (NRL) from 1936 through the end of World War II, the volume opens with a summary of the origins of that organization in the pre-World War I period. Other references to the early history of the laboratory are included at various points in the text and in the appendices.

The account includes a discussion of the relationships of the activity with the Secretary of the Navy, Bureau of Engineering, Bureau of Ships, and Office of Research and Inventions. At certain times during the laboratory's history these offices provided direction for NRL. The volume then relates the evolution of research policy and the liaison maintained with the Fleet, other services, universities, the National Defense Research Committee, and with British authorities. Thereafter, chapters are devoted to personnel and training matters, the laboratory's Department of Supplies and Accounts, and its Industrial Department. The latter department supported NRL's scientific work by maintaining facilities and shops, and by providing needed equipment.

In the final two chapters of the history, the activities of several subordinate commands and of the laboratory's scientific divisions are described in some detail. Included among the scientific divisions were those dealing with radio, sound, chemistry, optics, metallurgy, mechanics and electricity, and aircraft electrical programs.

The work includes a bibliography and appendices consisting of key documents, charts, rosters, and lists of NRL staff publications and patents. Footnotes in the text refer to these appendices and to other source materials.

Alfred T. Drury was the author of this history.

135.	Commandant Potomac River Naval Command, "Narrative History of the Potomac River Naval Command." Washington. 1945. 84 pp.

Late in 1941, the Commandant of the Washington Navy Yard was assigned as coordinator for the administration of most naval activities in the District of Columbia and in the Potomac River counties of Maryland and Virginia. In that capacity, this officer was designated Commandant of the Potomac River Naval Command.

This history traces the origins of the command from 1935, when initial proposals for its establishment were made, to the naval general order of 1941 forming the organization. Since the same general order established the Severn River Naval Command, some information on the origins of the latter activity also is included.

The balance of the account treats such topics as defense plans, the administration of Wave personnel, establishment of the Naval Barracks in Washington, expansion of the boundaries of the command, and the activities of various staff sections of the Potomac River Naval Command.

136.	Commandant Severn River Naval Command, "Administrative History of Severn River Naval Command." Annapolis, Maryland. 1946. 66 pp., appendices.

The Superintendent of the U. S. Naval Academy had the additional duty during World War II of commanding all naval activities in Anne Arundel County, Maryland. In addition to the academy, the components of this Severn River Naval Command included the Engineering Experiment Station, the Naval Radio Station, the Naval Hospital, the Postgraduate School, and the Supervisor of Shipbuilding, all of which were located in the Annapolis area.

The history includes separate chapters tracing the organization and functioning of each of these activities. In addition, it traces the origins of the Severn River Naval Command's headquarters and discusses the command's intelligence and security offices. Appendices include such items as air raid bills, organization charts, a list of courses taught by the Postgraduate School, and an enumeration of the ships contracted for under the direction of the Supervisor of Shipbuilding.

The author of this account was Louis H. Bolander.

137. Superintendent U. S. Naval Academy, "The United States Naval Academy and World War II." Annapolis, Maryland. 1946. 50 pp., appendices.

This relatively brief account initially concentrates on the effects of shortening the Naval Academy's course of instruction from four to three years due to wartime pressures. The text then discusses the problems associated with obtaining instructors during the war years, special training courses for naval reserve officers, and the operation of a reserve midshipmen school. The narrative concludes with comments on the construction of additional facilities at the academy, the World War II experiences of certain departments of the school, and recommendations regarding procedures in a future national emergency.

OPERATING FORCES

Atlantic

138.   Commander in Chief, U. S. Atlantic Fleet, "Commander in Chief, U. S. Atlantic Fleet," Vol. I (bound in 2 vols.). 1946. 785 pp., appendices, index.

The first volume of the Atlantic Fleet history focuses on operations, but provides considerable insight into policy, administrative, and logistical matters. Opening with a brief discussion of naval policy in the interwar years, the narrative recounts the establishment of the Atlantic Squadron in 1938 (which evolved into the Atlantic Fleet in 1941) and provides extensive details on operations and strategy during the period of American neutrality. Both in this period and in the years following American entry into World War II, much space is devoted to the campaign against the German U-boat, including details of such countermeasures as sonar, escort carriers, and convoy tactics.

Comprehensive accounts are included of the Allied amphibious operations in North Africa, Sicily, and Normandy. To provide background for these campaigns, the history also explores the development of amphibious tactics and landing craft, and discusses American planning for a second front in Europe.

A number of special topics are addressed, including the U. S. South Atlantic Force, Allied and enemy activities in Greenland, operations of German surface raiders and blockade runners, and the experiences of Atlantic Fleet ships attached to the British Home Fleet in 1942.

Appendices include detailed lists of enemy and American naval ships sunk in the theater, of Atlantic Fleet staff officers, and of the major type and task force commanders in the Atlantic.

139. Commander in Chief, U. S. Atlantic Fleet, "Commander Task Force Twenty-Four." Vol. II. 1946. 208 pp., appendices, index.

This narrative traces the wartime history of Task Force 24, which was the Support Force, Atlantic Fleet. The Support Force was established before the United States entered World War II in order to free the British from the primary responsibility for escort and protection of convoys between Great Britain and North America. The force continued to exercise this function after December 1941.

The well footnoted text contains a comprehensive description of war plans, convoy defense plans, combined command arrangements, and policy decisions that helped determine the successful outcome of the struggle against the German U-boat. The development of new tactics, weapons, detection devices, and their integration with established convoy defense procedures is described at length. The narrative also deals with the creation of bases to support the task force in both Canada and the British Isles, including St. John's, Halifax, Argentia, Gare Loch, and Londonderry.

The appendices consist of excerpts from pertinent task force operation plans.

140.	Commander in Chief, U. S. Atlantic Fleet, "Commander Greenland Patrol." Vol. III, 1946. 169 pp., appendix, index.

Organized in early 1941 to prevent the establishment of Axis air or naval bases in the area, the Greenland patrol force was composed initially of the Northeast Greenland Patrol and the South Greenland Patrol. The Command operated throughout World War II.

This narrative recounts the political and military events that led to the basing of American forces on the Danish island. Other subjects treated include the conduct of coastal patrols against German submarines and landing parties; relationships with the Coast Guard in its patrol of Greenland coastal waters and the Army in its construction of air installations; the establishment of radio, weather, and radar stations; and naval support for the massive ferrying of aircraft to Britain by way of Greenland in the buildup for the Normandy Invasion. Items of particular interest are the operations against the German weather stations on Shannon Island and Koldewey Island.

The text contains several photographs and the appendix consists of a 1942 survey of Greenland bases by Captain Robert B. Carney, USN, who then served as Chief of Staff to the Commander Support Force, Atlantic Fleet.

141.	Commander in Chief, U. S. Atlantic Fleet, "An Administrative History of Destroyers, Atlantic Fleet." Vol. VI. 1946. 80 pp., chronology, appendices.

This volume contains a short description of the wartime activities of the Atlantic Fleet type command responsible for destroyers, destroyer escorts, as well as all Coast Guard ships, as of January 1942. The text provides a chronological

119

summary of significant worldwide political and military events and also occurrences within the destroyer force from 1939 through 1945.

The narrative details the immediate prewar influx of ships and men into the Fleet and the changes in operations, training, and the command structure that ensued. As regards training, this history discusses the early wartime growth of Navy schools and efforts throughout the war to accommodate the program to new weapons, equipment, and tactics. Of particular interest is the destroyer command's participation in the Battle of the Atlantic prior to America's entry into the war, the bases for destroyers exchange, and the development of hunter-killer groups to combat the German "Schnorkel" submarines.

The appendices consist of compilations indicating the organization of Destroyers, Atlantic Fleet, by individual ships, divisions, and squadrons, at various times throughout World War II.

142.   Commander in Chief U. S. Atlantic Fleet, "Air Force Atlantic Fleet History." Vol. VII. Norfolk, Virginia. 1946. 208 pp., chronologies, appendices.

Divided into three chronological parts, this volume relates the history of the Atlantic Fleet naval air arm during the last three years of World War II. Each part consists of a detailed chronology of the year's occurrences, a topical treatment of the subject matter, and appendices reflecting organizational developments within the command.

The narrative sections treat such diverse facets of providing air support to the Fleet as the creation of new commands and subordinate units; the inception of new aircraft, weapons, and techniques to combat the Axis submarine threat; the promulgation of innovative plans and policies, the problems of aircraft maintenance, repair, and logistic support; the development of communications procedures; and the general administration of naval aviation in this particular theater of war.

Several photographs of Commander Air Force, Atlantic Fleet and his staff are located in the Part III narrative.

The voluminous appendices comprise tables, charts, graphs, and rosters representing the commissioning, decommissioning, reporting, designation, transfer, and detachment of air units, aircraft, and assigned support ships or craft. Aircraft strength figures, for the period covered by the history, are broken down according to type and by years, months, and days.

143. Commander in Chief, U. S. Atlantic Fleet, "Commander Fleet Operational Training Command." Vol. VIII. Norfolk, Virginia. 1946. 356 pp., appendices index.

Part I of this history is a topical discussion of the decision to establish the training command, which became operational in early 1943; measures taken to handle personnel for the rapidly expanded Fleet; the development of numerous East Coast bases as training sites; working relationships among the interdependent operational and type commands; and the organizational evolution of the Operation Training Command during the last three years of the war.

In Part II the various subordinate and geographically separate training installations are treated individually. The particular functions and responsibilities of each unit are dealt with at length. The schools provided instruction in such naval skills as antiaircraft and surface gunnery, net laying, minesweeping, and the many facets of antisubmarine warfare.

The appendices include organizational charts, a list of subordinate unit commanders, and a basic operation plan of the command for 1945.

144. Commander in Chief, U. S. Atlantic Fleet, "Administrative History of Commander Service Force, U.S. Atlantic Fleet, during World War II." Vol. IX. Norfolk, Virginia. 1946. 303 pp., appendices.

This administrative history is a comprehensive description of the role played by the Atlantic Fleet Service Force in the war. Comprising two narrative and two appendix sections, the volume details many aspects of providing naval logistic support.

Part I includes a thorough discussion of the organizational changes in the rapidly expanding Service Force from 1940 to the end of the war. The text recounts the effects on the command structure resulting from the early wartime burgeoning of the Fleet, the expansion of the area of responsibility, and the increase in operational requirements. To aid in tracing the organizational evolution of the force, flow charts are interspersed with the narrative.

The second part treats the various functions and duties of the command and its subordinate units. Responsibilities included maintaining ordnance; supervising Fleet communications; providing the operating forces with personnel and equipment; extending medical, recreational, financial, training, transportation, and administrative support; and supplying the operating forces with the materials needed to sustain them in combat.

The appendices contain pertinent letters,

memoranda, messages, and organizational tables.

The author of this work was Lieutenant Kenneth J. Ekdahl, (SC), USNR.

145.   Commander in Chief, U.S. Atlantic Fleet, "A History of the Amphibious Training Command, United States Atlantic Fleet and its Antecedent the Amphibious Force, United States Atlantic Fleet." Vol. X (bound in 3 vols.). Norfolk, Virginia. n.d. 872 pp., chronology.

In addition to relating the wartime activities of the Amphibious Training Command, and the Amphibious Force, from which the command evolved, this history discusses the evolution of amphibious doctrine during the prewar years. This detailed treatment focuses on the early efforts to adapt civilian-designed craft to amphibious warfare and to developing joint Army-Navy-Marine doctrine for landing troops on hostile shores. The conduct of landing exercises, as well as the planning for the North African Invasion, are described at length.

The account also deals with the training of naval personnel in the basic skills of amphibious warfare at East Coast schools. The text treats each amphibious training base individually and in detail while discussing such facets of the program as small boat handling, maintenance, and repair; loading, formation, and landing procedures; beach obstacle clearance actions; and small-caliber weapons operation.

The two narrative parts contain various relevant documents and the third section, a pictorial supplement, comprises approximately 400 photographs of key personnel, training facilities, landing exercises, and numerous types of amphibious ships and craft.

The authors of this work were Lieutenants

Hamilton S. Putnam, USNR, and Craig A. Livingston, USNR.

146. Commander in Chief, U. S. Atlantic Fleet, "Commander South Atlantic Force." Vol. XI. n.d. 245 pp., chronology.

Covering the period 1940 to 1945, this history details the wartime activities of the South Atlantic Force, which originally was designated Task Force 3 and later Task Force 23. Its successor organizations, Fourth Fleet and Task Force 27, also are discussed. The volume concentrates on the conduct of operations but also describes the command's administration.

Established to counter the Axis submarine threat to Allied convoy traffic and to protect that part of South America closest to Africa, the South Atlantic Force operated from bases in Brazil and Uruguay. The text discusses at length such aspects of the war at sea as the Neutrality Patrol, the air and surface campaign against German U-boats, and the support provided merchant ship convoys. The construction or development of bases in Brazil for attack and patrol aircraft, lighter-than-air craft, and surface ships is accorded emphasis. In this regard, political and military relations among U. S. Government, Navy, and Allied representatives and host country leaders are treated.

Numerous photographs are included of key personnel, as well as the facilities at Natal, Recife, Bahia, Belem, Fortaleza, and Amapa, Brazil, among others. Also included is a table indicating U-boats sunk by the Fourth Fleet during 1943 and 1944 indicating date, position, hull number, and attacking unit.

147.   Commander U. S. Naval Forces, Europe, "Administrative History, United States Naval Forces in Europe 1940-1946." Vols. I-VII (bound in 8 vols.). London. n.d. 2,856 pp., chronologies.

This voluminous study of U. S. Naval Forces, Europe consists of seven narrative volumes. A supplementary volume of documents is referred to but has not been located.

Volumes I and II treat the administrative activities of the command headquarters in London and its relationship with subordinate units. Separate parts in the volumes focus on topics of particular importance, such as the establishment of liaison between U. S. Navy and British authorities in Great Britain during 1940; the organizational development of the headquarters staff; the control of task forces in European waters; planning and preparation for the Normandy Invasion (Operation OVERLORD); the creation of naval bases and facilities in the British Isles, France, and Germany; and naval administration in occupied Germany and Austria during 1945 and early 1946.

Volume III describes the work of the hydrographic, navigation, medical, chaplain, technical intelligence, postal, and communications functions associated with the command, as well as the activities of the Naval Attache, London.

The supply and logistic support of American and Allied naval forces in Europe, including the lend-lease program and the supply of cross-channel operations from bases in the United Kingdom, is dealt with in Volume IV.

Volume V provides a comprehensive and detailed account of the naval preparations for the Normandy landing and the conduct of the operation. A separate index is attached to this volume.

Naval planning for the post-hostilities occupation of Germany and Austria and for naval representation in the liberated areas of

Scandinavia, the Low Countries, and France is the subject of Volume VI. Specific parts deal with the organization of U. S. Naval Forces, Germany (Task Force 124), and U. S. Ports and Bases, Germany (Task Force 126), the preparation of naval personnel for occupation duty, and naval representation on the Control Council, Germany.

In Volume VII, the narrative covers the actions of subordinate commands such as Task Force 124; Task Force 126; the naval contingents of the Control Council, Germany; the Allied Commission, Austria; the Allied Missions to Scandinavia and the Low Countries; U. S. Naval Forces, Azores; and U. S. Naval Forces, Mediterranean.

Accompanying the text are tables, plans, correspondence, maps, and photographs.

148. Commander U. S. Naval Forces, Northwest African Waters, "Naval Forces, Northwest African Waters and the Eighth Fleet." 5 vols. 1945. 176 pp., appendices, bibliographical note.

This organization participated in the major Mediterranean naval campaigns during the last years of World War II. The command was organized in March 1943 as the Eighth Fleet and initially was responsible to the Commander in Chief, U. S. Fleet for naval administration and to the Naval Deputy of the Commander in Chief, Allied Forces, for naval operations.

The history comprises two narrative volumes and three volumes of appendices. The latter comprise detailed action reports for the Sicily, Salerno, and Southern France landings.

The first volume is arranged topically and concentrates on the administration of American naval forces in the Mediterranean. The first of three parts in this volume provides a chronological treatment of the command's activities, as well as a discussion of problems encountered and conclusions drawn. The second part deals with planning, personnel administration, communications, and intelligence. The final section consists of appended letters, directives, and messages of importance.

The establishment of naval bases in North Africa, Sicily, Corsica, Sardinia, and on the Italian mainland to support the command's Mediterranean operations is dealt with in the second volume. Also discussed are the workings of the Eighth Fleet logistic system in the provision of such items as construction materials, expendable supplies, equipment, weapons, ammunition, vehicles, and spare parts to the operating forces.

Commander Julian M. Boit, USNR, and Lieutenant Commander Carl Bridenbaugh, USNR, authored the first volume. The second volume was completed by Commander Melvin F. Talbot, (SC), USN, and Lieutenant Commander James C. Risk, USNR.

Pacific

149.   Commander in Chief, U. S. Pacific Fleet, "Commander in Chief, United States Pacific Fleet and Pacific Ocean Areas, Command History." 3 vols. 1946. 419 pp., appendices.

Composed of one narrative volume and two volumes of appendices, this work details the administrative conduct of the war in the Pacific at both the joint and fleet command level.

Following a discussion of inter-service and

intra-service command relationships and the wartime organizational development of the staff for this command, the text describes the functions of separate divisions and sections within the headquarters. The activity of the Operations Division in coordinating air and surface actions, troop movements, and in insuring the combat readiness of units is recounted. Combat, strategic, radio, and photographic intelligence collection techniques, as well as psychological warfare methods, are related. Other major topics include the provision of logistic support to the operating forces; strategic planning and the formulation of war plans; and the utilization of the various modes of military communication. Also discussed are the diverse functions of the Administration Division, which had cognizance over awards, postal matters, military government, public information, censorship, welfare and recreation, and voting.

The first appendix volume consists of organizational charts, graphs, tables, and photographs of naval leaders and headquarters facilities in Guam and Hawaii.

The second appendix volume contains flow charts, staff instructions, personnel rosters, telephone directories, sample forms, studies, letters, and memoranda.

150. Commander in Chief, U. S. Pacific Fleet, "History of the Amphibious Forces, U. S. Pacific Fleet." 4 vols. 1945. 1,892 pp., glossaries.

This narrative history provides a comprehensive account of the command that conducted a number of major amphibious operations in the Pacific.

The first volume focuses on the development of amphibious forces from the prewar years of experimentation with new concepts and training through the wartime years of operational application. The headquarters staff sections, among them operations, gunnery, force control, supply and logistics, pontoons, aerology, and maintenance, are treated individually. The final section of text provides a discussion of problems encountered and suggested solutions. Appended documents include an organizational description of the Amphibious Forces as of August 1945.

The second volume contains separate historical accounts of subordinate amphibious groups and transport squadrons.

In volume three the text details the wartime work of the Administrative Command, Amphibious Forces with emphasis on the structural evolution of the organization. Also individually treated are the Administrative Command, Amphibious Forces, U. S. Pacific Fleet, Marianas and the training facilities located in the Hawaiian Islands.

The fourth volume relates the activities of the Training Command, Amphibious Forces in providing the Fleet with personnel instructed in the techniques of amphibious warfare. The narrative is divided into three parts which consist of a brief chronological summary of the command's history, a discussion of each staff section's functions, and appended material on the training bases at Coronado and Port Hueneme, California.

Volume four also contains the historical submissions of Commander Air Support Control Units and Commander Underwater Demolition Teams, both of which were components of Amphibious Forces, U. S. Pacific Fleet.

Photographs of commanders, amphibious craft, combat actions, and training facilities, as well as charts, tables, maps, correspondence, sample forms, manuals, and blueprints of training facilities, are included in the text. A glossary of abbreviations and a listing of Pacific place names follow the fourth volume.

151. Commander in Chief, U. S. Pacific Fleet, "Administrative Study of Commander Destroyer/Cruisers Pacific Fleet during World War II." 1946. 289 pp., appendices, bibliographical note, index.

This narrative systematically relates the wartime functions of the cruiser-destroyer type command. The first chapter recounts the organizational development of the headquarters staff. Succeeding chapters treat aspects of the command's mission.

The subjects covered include training in antisubmarine warfare, communication procedures, gunnery, and torpedo warfare. The text also discusses the workings of the Combat Information Center, established to provide tactical and technical information to the ships of the command; and the Forward Area Representatives, who dealt directly with the operating forces for the type commander. Logistics, intelligence, personnel matters, and training are discussed separately.

Photographs depicting ships and facilities of the command are interspersed within the text, and appendix documents, consisting of staff instructions, flow charts, graphs, memoranda, site plans, training curricula, and publications follow several chapters.

The authors of the history were Lieutenant Commander Robert M. Lunny, USNR, Lieutenant Thomas N. Newell, USNR, and Lieutenant (junior grade) Howard J. Thompson, USNR.

152. Commander in Chief, U. S. Pacific Fleet, "History of the Fleet Operational Training Command, Pacific." 2 vols. 1946. 870 pp., appendices.

Organized according to command structure, these volumes include an overall history of the

Fleet Operational Training Command and separate narratives submitted by subordinate functions.

The description of the parent organization, which was charged with the responsibility for training crews of ships to be commissioned and those already in service, covers relationships with operating forces and shore establishment commands; the composition and development of the headquarters staff; logistic support of the scattered training facilities; and the conduct of precommissioning, shakedown, and refresher training programs, as well as training in gunnery, ship defense, and antisubmarine warfare.

The remainder of the first volume and all of the second comprise histories of subordinate training activities located on the West Coast. These commands included the Escort Carrier Pre-Commissioning School at Puget Sound Navy Yard, Washington; the Anti-Aircraft and Small Craft schools at Pacific Beach and San Pedro, California; and the Shakedown, Sound, and Combat Information Center Indoctrination schools at San Diego, California.

Photographs of training operations and facilities, organizational charts, correspondence, maps, and site plans are interspersed in the text.

The appendices, which follow many of the separate parts, are composed of training instructions, operation plans, tables, sample forms, site plans, flow charts, and publications.

153.   Commander in Chief, U. S. Pacific Fleet, "Administrative History of Minecraft Pacific Fleet." 1946. 215 pp., appendices.

This one-volume narrative treats the administrative activities of the senior minecraft commands in the Pacific. During the prewar years, mine warfare responsibilities were handled by

Minecraft, Battle Force and Train Squadron Six. In the early war years, these commands were combined to form Service Squadron Six. From October 1944 to the end of World War II, Commander Minecraft, U. S. Pacific Fleet functioned as the type command.

The text describes the missions, force composition, doctrine, staff organization, and defensive employment of the minecraft commands prior to the Pearl Harbor Attack and in the early phase of the Pacific campaign. The growth and development of minecraft forces and mine warfare techniques are given considerable attention, with particular emphasis on such aspects as minesweeping and minelaying procedures, degaussing, mine disarming, mine modification and experimentation, conversion of destroyers to minelayers, net and boom laying, the acquisition and integration into the Fleet of new types of minecraft, and aerial mining. The two major subordinate components of the Commander Minecraft, U. S. Pacific Fleet headquarters--the Operating Staff and the Administrative Command--are dealt with separately and in detail. Topics discussed include amphibious assault planning, joint operations, ship readiness, and logistic support.

Combined with the narrative are flow charts, correspondence, and tables. Footnotes indicate documentation for much of the work.

The appendices contain staff instructions and several organizational diagrams.

154. Commander in Chief, U. S. Pacific Fleet, "Motor Torpedo Boat Squadrons." 2 vols. n.d. 265 pp., appendix, index.

Comprising one narrative volume and one volume of appendices, this history thoroughly details the wartime administration of Motor Torpedo Boat Squadrons, U. S. Pacific Fleet, and of similar units assigned to the Commander, Southwest Pacific Area.

The text is divided in five parts, the first of which describes the activities of motor torpedo boat forces prior to the establishment of the type command in February 1944. Parts II and III discuss the early development of the organization and its relationships with Commander Motor Torpedo Boat Squadrons, South Pacific Area and Commander Naval Forces, Northern Solomons. The latter commands for the most part exercised the type command function during 1944 and the first quarter of 1945. The section contains information on the organization and functioning of the headquarters staff, operational procedures, the training program, and aspects of logistic support concerned with spare parts, fuel, bases, and shipping. In Part IV the narrative treats the development of the type command during 1945 when Commander Motor Torpedo Boat Squadrons, U. S. Pacific Fleet became responsible for all boat activities in the Pacific theater. The final part contains an analysis of command problems encountered in the war and a brief conclusion.

The appendix volume includes war diaries, staff instructions, tables, operation plans, maps, and correspondence relating to the administration of the motor torpedo boat forces.

155. Commander in Chief, U. S. Pacific Fleet, "History of Service Force," 1946. 389 pp.

The history of Service Force, U. S. Pacific Fleet is arranged according to the organizational structure of the command.

The opening chapter traces the functional development of the type command (initially designated Base Force, U. S. Pacific Fleet) from early

1941 through August 1945. Responses to the growth of the Fleet and the demands of wartime operations are described. The workings of headquarters sections which administered such diverse Fleet functions as photographic, chaplain, maintenance, personnel, postal, printing, and shore patrol support, are detailed. Other important subdivisions were the Advanced Base Section, the Area Petroleum Office, and the Fleet Training Center, Oahu, Hawaii.

The activities of the units which directly supplied the Fleet--Service Squadrons Two, Three, Four, Six, Seven, Eight, Nine, Ten, Twelve, and Fourteen--are recounted. The text also describes operations involving salvage, repair, hydrographic surveying, towing service, and the installation of underwater harbor defenses.

The narrative history is well footnoted and several photographs of Service Force commanders and headquarters facilities are appended.

156. Commander in Chief, U. S. Pacific Fleet, "Administrative History of the North Pacific Area." 1945. 302 pp.

This history recounts the growth of the naval establishment in Alaska from the period between the wars to the end of World War II. The narrative treats the evolution of the command structure, including the creation, administration, staff functioning, and operational activities of the Alaskan Sector, 13th Naval District; the Northwest Sea Frontier; the North Pacific Force and Area; the 17th Naval District; and the Alaskan Sea Frontier. Other topics include the development of war plans for the defense of Alaska, the attacks on Attu and Kiska, and for a proposed invasion of the Kurile Islands; the relationships between Army and Navy commands in Alaska; the construction, logistic support, and operation of naval air stations, surface patrol bases, and aerological stations at such locations as Sitka, Kodiak, Dutch Harbor, Adak, Juneau, Seward, Amchitka, and Port Armstrong; the joint operation against the Japanese occupation forces on Attu and Kiska; and the Japanese air attack on Dutch Harbor.

The text is well footnoted and contains photographs of installations, flow charts, and tables showing the composition of forces.

157.   Commander in Chief, U. S. Pacific Fleet, "Administrative History of the ComMarGils Area." 6 vols. 1946. 1,835 pp., chronology, appendix.

Comprising five narrative parts and one appendix section, this voluminous work thoroughly details the wartime administrative history of naval forces in the Marshall and Gilbert islands. The Marshalls-Gilberts Area command was established in October 1944.

Part I contains a description of the geography and early history of the area. It also provides an operational summary of the Gilberts Campaign of 1943, focusing on the landings and naval air actions, and the Marshall Campaign in early 1944, including individual treatment of the attacks on Majuro, Roi-Namur, Kwajalein, and Eniwetok. The following sections deal in depth with the organizational evolution of Commander Marshalls-Gilberts Area (Commander Task Force 96) and the Navy's management of civil affairs.

The second part explores the varied activities and functions of four major subordinate organizations within Task Force 96--the Shore Based Air Force, the Defense and Service Force, the Patrol and Escort Group, and the Utility Group.

Part III concentrates on the role of the headquarters staff, including the responsibilities and procedures of each subdivision. The administration, personnel, operations, logistics, communications, construction, medical, military government, and aviation material sections are covered.

Part IV of the text discusses the separate island and atoll commands, summarizing their activities in base development, headquarters organization, port operation, air and shore defense, military government, personnel administration, training, joint operations, logistics, and postwar planning. The physical characteristics of each of the atolls treated, as well as the makeup of their populations, are described briefly.

The final part details the workings of each of the subordinate entities within the island and atoll commands, including their personnel, medical, communications, intelligence, chaplain, supply, ordnance, aerological, maintenance, and legal sections. The functioning of attached Army engineer, communication, port and service, weather station, and air transport command units, as well as Coast Guard and Marine organizations, is explored.

The appendix volume contains numerous letters, instructions, directives, studies, unit composition tables, operation orders and plans, maps, site plans, and photographs relating to all facets of Commander Marshalls-Gilberts Area activities.

Flow charts, maps, rosters, hydrographic charts, a chronology, and photographs of facilities, personnel, and enemy fortifications also accompany the text.

Lieutenant Hollice E. Stevenson, USNR, and Lieutenant (junior grade) Ralph D. Spencer, USNR, are identified as two of the authors of the history.

158.   Commander in Chief, U. S. Pacific Fleet, "Administrative History of the Forward Area, Central Pacific and the Marianas Area." 1946. 194 pp., appendices, index.

Established in February 1944, Commander Forward Area, Central Pacific became Commander Marianas Area in June 1945 and retained that title for the remainder of the war. This narrative discusses the command's activities in administering the Gilbert, Marshall, and Mariana Island groups, as well as the Iwo Jima and the Ellice Island areas.

The text is divided both topically and according to command structure. Subjects covered include the area's geographical and climatalogical character, the development of the headquarters staff, measures taken to defend the islands, the conduct of offensive operations, and the utilization of aircraft for air-sea rescue, transportation, and logistic support. In the organizational section, the narrative treats the sections within the command which dealt with base development, military government, shipping control, gunnery, supply, postal affairs, surface operations, air operations, and public information, as well as the individual atoll and island commands.

The appendices comprise biographies of commanding officers, general descriptions of several major islands, extensive correspondence, charts, operation plans and orders, rosters, maps, flow charts, and photographs of personnel and naval facilities.

159.   Commander in Chief, U. S. Pacific Fleet, "Commander U. S. Naval Forces, Southwest Pacific." n.d. 210 pp., appendix.

This history of the wartime administration of U. S. Naval Forces in the Southwest Pacific is arranged topically.

American naval forces in the area initially were assigned to the American, British, Dutch, Australian Area (ABDA) command, and then to the Australia-New Zealand Area (ANZAC) command. In April 1942, they came under General Douglas MacArthur, who served as Commander in Chief, Southwest Pacfiic Area. In February 1943, naval forces in the area were designated the Seventh Fleet.

Much of the text is devoted to a discussion of Navy interaction with Allied and Army commanders and forces in these various organizations. Particular treatment is given to combined and joint activity in amphibious, air, and logistic matters. The narrative also details the history of naval commands in the theater, the organizational evolution of the headquarters staff, and the development of such subordinate administrative commands as the Southwest Pacific Sea Frontier and the Philippine Sea Frontier.

Other topics separately dealt with include the testing and standardization of amphibious landing techniques, the conduct of amphibious warfare, the use of submarines to support guerrilla actions in the Philippines, and the functioning of the naval intelligence center.

The appendix consists of selected messages and correspondence.

Sea Frontiers and Operating Bases

160.   Commander Caribbean Sea Frontier, "Administrative History of the Caribbean Sea Frontier to VE-Day." 1945. 44 pp., appendices, bibliography.

This history traces the development of the Caribbean Sea Frontier which evolved from the Tenth Naval District and the Caribbean Naval Coastal Frontier commands. The narrative is divided chronologically, but each section contains topical subheadings.

The subjects treated include the organizational development of the command and its subordinate sectors--Puerto Rico, Trinidad, Guantanamo, and Aruba-Curacao; relationships with the British, Dutch, and French Allies in regard to the disposition of their Caribbean possessions; measures taken to improve operations with Army and Coast Guard forces; the establishment of air and surface bases in Cuba, the French Antilles, the British West Indies, and the Netherlands West Indies; and the conduct of the command's major function, the war against German U-boats.

The narrative contains maps indicating boundaries with other American and Allied commands and tables depicting merchant ship losses.

Appended to the text are a bibliography, a chronicle of Tenth Naval District activities, descriptions of wartime activities on Antigua, British West Indies, and a table showing the number and type of ships and craft assigned to the Caribbean Sea command fron December 1941 to July 1945.

161.   Commander Eastern Sea Frontier, "History of the Eastern Sea Frontier (Organizational and Operational)." New York, New York. 67 pp.

This brief account summarizes the activities of the primary naval command responsible for the defense of the East Coast of the United States and for the protection of shipping in the area's coastal waters. The Commandant of the Third Naval District served as the Sea Frontier's commander.

The history traces the evolution of this command from 1940, at which time it was known as the North Atlantic Naval Coastal Frontier, through the end of the war. Details on the frontier's relationships with naval districts and with Army commands in the area are included. The balance of the account concentrates on the organization, employment, and doctrine of the naval surface and air forces assigned to the command.

162.   Commander Gulf Sea Frontier, "History of the Gulf Sea Frontier, 6 February 1942-14 August 1945." Miami, Florida. 1946. 337 pp., chronology, appendices.

Established in early 1942, the command's primary role was antisubmarine warfare. This history provides a chronological account of the fight against the German U-boats in the Gulf of Mexico, including a detailed rendition of events and significant operational decisions.

The text also treats separately several topics of importance, among them the organizational development of the sea frontier and its two major subordinate commands, the Seventh and Eighth Naval Districts; the functioning and structure of the sea frontier staff; the control and routing of shipping; the construction of advanced bases in Cuba and the British West Indies; the establishment of a tactical Radio Direction Finder net; development of the subordinate Coast Guard Anti-Submarine Flotilla; naval relations with Cuba; communications; personnel matters; and planning for the postwar defense of the Gulf.

The appendices consist of a list of Allied ships sunk, with date, place, and time of loss indicated; a narrative description of facilities consolidation and reduction measures taken in the latter part of the war; a list of successful attacks on German submarines, also with date, time, and place indicated; a table showing the composition of Gulf Sea Frontier task forces; and a summary of achievements by the Operations Research Group, a body of civilian technical and scientific advisors. Both the text and the appendix section contain flow charts, maps, hyrographic charts, tables, graphs, and pertinent directives.

The author of this history was Lieutenant Jack A. Reynolds, USNR.

163. Commander Western Sea Frontier, "Administrative History of Western Sea Frontier during World War II." 7 vols. San Francisco, California. 1946. 898 pp., appendices, list of abbreviations.

Responsible for the sea defense of the Pacific coast of the United States and Mexico, the Western Sea Frontier was comprised of many forces and commands, including the Eleventh, Twelfth, and Thirteenth Naval Districts. The text of this history is divided into two general categories: operations against the enemy in coastal waters and direction of the West Coast logistic effort in support of the Pacific operating forces. In each major part the narrative treats the functions of the staff sections within the Commander Western Sea Frontier headquarters.

Part I contains an introductory description of the origins and establishment of the command. It then turns to discussions of the composition of surface and air units, the organization of coastal sectors, and the work of the Operations, Planning, Intelligence, Communications, Air Office, and Shipping Control sections of the operational staff.

Part II traces the wartime evolution of the administrative command structure developed for the control of logistics activities. Such aspects as the procurement and disposition of resources, industrial relations, ship maintenance, Fleet base and advanced base development, air and surface transportation and supply, personnel distribution, public relations, aerology, and convoy routing and defense are covered.

The text of the two narrative volumes contains maps, organization charts, and diagrams.

The five appendix volumes consist of pertinent letters, memoranda, manuals, orders, operation plans, rosters, reports, instructions, conference minutes, unit histories, and statistical analyses.

The author of the work was Lieutenant Commander Philip S. Klein, USNR.

164. Commander Caribbean Sea Frontier, "Aruba-Curacao Command Headquarters, Commander All Forces." Willemstad, Netherlands West Indies. 1945. 57 pp., bibliography, appendices.

Established in early 1942 to defend the oil refineries and storage facilities of the Netherlands West Indies and to expedite the flow of petroleum products to Allied forces, Commander All Forces, Aruba-Curacao, continued to function in this capacity for the remainder of the war. The history recounts this unique naval command's activities in directing the efforts of American, British, and Dutch naval, air, and land units. Because of the international and joint service composition of the command, much emphasis is given to relationships with these entities. Dealings with civilian authorities on the islands also are discussed. Among other topics treated are the development of the organization's structure, the strategic value of Aruba and Curacao, and the construction of naval facilities. Also described is naval supervision and control of fuel supply, including the loading, discharging, repair, and armed guard support of tankers, as well as the formation, routing, escort protection, and harbor security of convoys.

The text contains aerial photographs of facilities, fuel distribution charts, and maps.

The appendix documents consist of orders, letters, statistical charts, memoranda, regulations, maps, and ocean charts.

The authors of this work were Lieutenant Commanders Robert H. Connery, USNR, and Marion V. Brewington, USNR.

165. Commander Caribbean Sea Frontier, "The Guantanamo Sector, Caribbean Sea Frontier and the U. S. Naval Operating Base, Guantanamo Bay, Cuba." 2 vols. 1945. 458 pp., appendices, bibliography, list of abbreviations.

The narrative volume provides a detailed description of the Navy's wartime activities in Cuba, Jamaica, Haiti, and contiguous waters. Charged with directing the operations of all undersea, surface, and air forces assigned to the command and with formulating operational policy, Commander Guantanamo Sector additionally served as Commander Naval Operating Base in administering the shore establishment. The latter consisted of the Naval Station, Naval Air Station, Net Depot, and Marine Corps Base at Guantanamo.

Arranged according to organizational structure, the text treats separately the subordinate entities within the dual command, which handled such varied functions as shipping control, intelligence collection and analysis, liaison with other services and foreign governments, communications, base defense, port security, base and facilities construction, training, ship repair, medical support, surplus materials disposition, and the many facets of logistic support. Particular attention is devoted to the administration of naval air, inshore patrol, and convoy escort forces.

The appendix volume contains ocean charts, maps, flow charts, statistical tables, graphs, memoranda, letters, reports, and photographs representing installations, training operations, harbor defenses, and naval personnel.

166.   Commander Caribbean Sea Frontier, "An Administrative History of the U. S. Naval Operating Base Trinidad, B. W. I. and the Trinidad Sector of the Caribbean Sea Frontier, 7 December 1941 to August 1945." 195 pp., chronology, appendices.

The text of this history details the wartime administration of the dual command, based in Trinidad, British West Indies, whose primary responsibility was antisubmarine warfare. The narrative is divided into four distinct parts.

Part I relates the establishment of the Trinidad Sector, its assigned duties, organization, and position in the command structure with respect to the Caribbean Sea Frontier and the Tenth Naval District. Also discussed are relationships with the Army and with British air, ground, and naval forces in planning for defense of the operational area.

Part II comprises a chronology of significant events occurring between February 1941 and August 1945.

The Naval Base at Trinidad is the subject of Part III. This part includes a description of the island's topography and people, the development of the naval installation, and the functioning of subordinate departments concerned with personnel, harbor defense, shakedown training, communications, intelligence, supply, and medical matters.

The final section covers the Navy's joint use of Army air bases and the activities of outlying installations, including those in Trinidad Island, British Guiana, Saint Lucia Island (also a British possession), and Surinam (Dutch).

Both the text and the appendix section contain hydrographic charts, maps, site plans, reports, letters, minutes of meetings, orders, plans, tables, and photographs of key naval personnel, base and port facilities, harbor defenses, living quarters, and airfields.

The authors of this work were Lieutenant Commanders Robert F. Millett, USNR, and Kenneth S. Wales, USNR.

167. Commander in Chief, U. S. Atlantic Fleet, "Commandant N. O. B. Bermuda." Vol. V. Bermuda. 1946. 84 pp., chronology, appendices.

The American military presence in Bermuda, beginning in 1941 and continuing through the war, is examined in this history. The narrative deals at length with such subjects as the extensive diplomatic activity between American and British officials preceding the actual basing of American forces on the island; the construction of air, land, and sea facilities and the dredging of a deep-draft channel; the relationships among the various naval commands in Bermuda and other Allied armed forces; the organizational development and composition of the Naval Operating Base, Bermuda; the training and other logistic-type services provided the Atlantic Fleet; and dealings with the civilian labor force on Bermuda.

The text contains many aerial photographs

of naval installations, key personnel, and training operations, as well as several maps and charts of the island.

The appendices consist of a listing by project number of facilities constructed, with their completion dates; the base agreement authorizing the stationing of U. S. forces in Bermuda; a compilation of submarine sightings and anti-submarine measures taken; a list of key Allied military and civilian personnel; and a short chronology representing major wartime events concerning the island.

168. Commander in Chief, U. S. Atlantic Fleet, "Naval Operating Base, Iceland." Vol. IV. Reykjavik, Iceland. 1946. 107 pp.

The wartime history of Naval Operating Base, Iceland is described in detail in this narrative summary. Particular emphasis is given to the military and political circumstances surrounding the establishment of American bases on the island and the occupation by U. S. armed forces. The influence of Iceland on United States' war plans also is discussed.

The construction or enlargement of facilities, such as the air base, tank farm, salvage depot, ammunition depot, billets, warehouses, and defensive works, needed to support the operating forces, is accorded attention. The text thoroughly treats the subject of Army-Navy, inter-Allied, and Allied-Iceland cooperation in the functioning of the naval operating base. Further, the development of command relationships and organizational procedures within this naval command are detailed.

The text is fully footnoted and contains several relevant documentary extracts as well as numerous aerial photographs depicting facilities at coastal and inland naval installations.

169.   Commandant Eleventh Naval District, "Administrative History of the Naval Operating Base, Terminal Island (San Pedro), California." San Pedro, California. 1946. 635 pp.

Divided into seven chapters, the history of the naval operating base at Terminal Island comprehensively treats the command's wartime administrative activities.

Chapter I relates the origins and organizational development of the base command and the headquarters staff from June 1940 to the end of the war. The text deals with such matters as staff reorganizations, position title changes, and relationships with subordinate offices.

In Chapter II, the narrative discusses separately the staff branches reponsible for operations, liaison with the forces afloat, ship commissioning, legal affairs, fire protection, training and education, historical matters, public relations, and damage control.

The third section describes the work of subordinate activities, including the Small Craft T ining Center, the Naval Personnel Center, the Naval Drydocks, the Naval Receiving Station and Disciplinary Barracks, the Naval Fuel Annex, the Target Repair Base, the Naval Net Depot, the Naval Firefighters School, and the Wartime Merchant Ship Communications School, all of which were located at San Pedro, California; naval activities at Port Hueneme, California; the Naval Fuel Annex at Elk Hills, California; the aviation facilities at Litchfield Park, Arizona, and Terminal Island and Los Alamitos, California; and the medical activities at Long Beach, San Pedro, and Corona, California.

Chapters IV through VII cover the subjects

of security and local defense, transportation, housing, and civilian personnel, respectively.

Listings of sources used in writing this history follow each chapter.

The author of this account was Lieutenant Commander Hubert B. Rouse, USNR.

Topical Histories

170. Commander Submarine Force, U. S. Atlantic Fleet, "Submarine Commands." Vols. I-II. 1946. 672 pp.

Due to the interdependence of the three major submarine commands of World War II, the authors of this account combined their administrative histories into a single narrative. The project was under the overall direction of Captain Richard G. Voge, USN, who also prepared sections relating to the Submarine Force, Pacific Fleet. Lieutenant Commander Donald S. Graham, USN and Commander William H. Hazzard, USN, respectively, prepared the materials relating to Submarines Atlantic Fleet and Submarines Southwest Pacific.

Volume I begins with separate discussions of the administration of Submarines, Atlantic Fleet; Submarine Force, Pacific Fleet; and Submarines, Southwest Pacific. Separate topical chapters then relate the experiences of all these commands in the areas of selecting and training submarine personnel; medical, health, and morale programs; awards and citations; and submarine publicity.

Volume II continues to provide topical

coverage. These subjects include discussions of the development of submarine types and equipment, research and development and operations research, communications, submarine construction at specific naval and private yards, transfers of submarines to Great Britian, maintenance, and logistics. The narrative concludes with sections describing twenty-two separate bases used by American submarines throughout the world. These facilities ranged from major activities such as New London, Connecticut and Pearl Harbor, to more minor bases such as Dutch Harbor, Alaska and Surabaya, Java.

Reference is made to a volume containing documentary annexes to the history. However, an appendix volume has not been located.

171. Office of Naval History, "An Administrative History of PT's in World War II." Washington. 1946. 222 pp., appendices.

In addition to describing the Navy's motor torpedo boat program, the authors of this history evaluate the difficulties confronted and offer "alternate suggestions which would be helpful in the event that it was again necessary to set up a special program."

The history initially discusses the development and testing of motor torpedo boats in the United States during the prewar and early World War II years. It then turns to a discussion of the Motor Torpedo Boat Squadrons Training Center at Melville, Rhode Island, which was responsible for instructing PT officers and men; the PT Shakedown Detail in Miami, Florida; and the PT Commissioning Details in the New York and New Orleans areas. A chapter follows describing the activities of the U. S. Naval Station, Taboga, Panama, which overhauled PT boats and provided operational training for their crews. The history concludes with an account of the development and use of MTB tender ships.

Appendices include details on the PT building program, personnel distribution, and operational losses.

The authors of this history were Frank A. Tredinnick, Jr., and Harrison L. Bennett.

172. Office of the Chief of Naval Operations, "Arming of Merchant Ships and Naval Armed Guard Service." Washington. 1946. 282 pp., appendices.

This study focuses on the Armed Guard Program, through which guns and gun crews were placed on board merchant ships as protection against enemy attack. The narrative begins with a brief description of the administrative machinery and the problems involved in the operation of the program. The following two chapters discuss in detail the selection, training, and assignment of officer and enlisted personnel, and the effort to arm and equip merchant ships for defense against air, surface, and submarine attack. In a short epilogue, the process of disarming merchant ships is reviewed. A series of eleven appendices includes statistical tables, charts, and graphs.

173. Office of the Chief of Naval Operations, "History of the Naval Armed Guard Afloat, World War II." Washington. 1946. 253 pp.

Originally written to accompany the preceding volume as an operational history of the Armed Guard Service, this manuscript covers all theaters of war from North Russia to the Indian Ocean. Representative engagements in which the Armed Guard participated are detailed. According

to the author, Lieutenant (junior grade) William
C. Askew, USNR, the study utilized the complete
files of the Armed Guard Service. Included
with the manuscript is an extensive commentary
by Lieutenant Francis L. Berkeley, Jr., USNR,
who reviewed the work in 1949.

APPENDIX A

INDIVIDUALS ASSIGNED TO ADMINISTRATIVE HISTORY
PROJECT, JUNE 4, 1945

Secretary of the Navy and Executive Office of the
 Secretary

    Secretary of the Navy   Dr. Robert G. Albion
    Procurement   LCDR R. H. Connery
    Judge Advocate General
    Public Relations   Mr. George Marvin
    Office of Procurement   LCDR R. H. Connery
     and Material
    General Counsel   LCDR R. H. Connery
    Fiscal Director Budget
    Administrative Office   LT R. D. Hubbard
    Research and Develop-
     ment
    Civilian Personnel   Dr. Robert G. Albion
        LT (j.g.) J. E. McLean

Commander in Chief, United
 States Fleet   LCDR W. M. Whitehill

Chief of Naval Operations

    Central Divsion   LT E. E. Morison
        LT D. S. Ballantine
        LT M. P. Gilmore
        LT John H. Gleason

    Hydrographic Office   LT (j.g.) O. E. Klapp
    Naval Air Transport   LT (j.g.) Louise T.
     Service   Stockly
    Naval Communication   LT (j.g.) Meta A. Ennis
     Division
    Office of Naval   LCDR G. P. Simons
     Intelligence   LT W. S. Thomas
        LT W. T. Jones

<u>Deputy Chief of Naval Operations (Air)</u>	LT (j.g.) Henry M. Dater LT (j.g.) Adrian Van Wyen LT (j.g.) William G. Land LT (j.g.) George H. Wright 2nd LT Edna L. Smith 2nd LT Anne Fortune Vaupel
<u>Bureau of Aeronautics</u>	LT C. L. Lord LT (j.g.) C. F. Stanwood LT Albert R. Buchanan LT (j.g.) Andrew R. Hilen, Jr. ENS Florence E. Arvidson LT (j.g.) W. O. Shanahan LT Peter Cary
<u>Bureau of Medicine and Surgery</u>	LT Chester L. Guthrie LT (j.g.) Robert L. Thompson ENS Harold S. Schultz
<u>Bureau of Naval Personnel</u>	LT J. W. Hurst LT John Marion LT E. D. H. Johnson LT Sherman Hayden LT Russell H. Seibert
<u>Bureau of Ordnance</u>	LT Joseph J. Mathews LT Thomas B. Rowland LT (j.g.) Winchester H. Heicher
<u>Bureau of Ships</u>	LT Paul J. Strayer LCDR George A. Andrews LT Clarence D. Long
<u>Bureau of Supplies and Accounts</u>	LT James Colvin LT Mark W. Alger ENS T. J. Graves
<u>Bureau of Yards and Docks and the Civil Engineer Corps</u>	LCDR Frank W. Herring LCDR E. R. Peters LT R. H. Dodds LT H. R. Fairbanks ENS V. R. Graves

<u>Atlantic Fleet</u>	LCDR Frank L. R. Thompson
AirLant	LT George H. Markham
DesLant	LT Winston LaBarre
SubsLant	————
PhibLant	LT H. S. Putnam
	LT C. A. Livingston
ServLant	LT K. J. Ekdahl
COTCLant	LT E. J. Kemler
<u>Pacific Fleet</u>	LCDR J. H. Kemble
	LT E. T. James, Assistant
AirPac	LCDR A. D. Lindley
CruDesPac	————
SubsPac	————
PhibPac	————
ServPac	————
COTCPac	————
Marianas	
Marshalls-Gilberts	LT Hollice E. Stevenson
<u>Sea Frontiers</u>	
Eastern	LCDR L. R. Thompson
Gulf	LT J. A. Reynolds
Caribbean	LT M.T. Patten
Panama	LT Leo J. Roland
Western	LT P. S. Klein
Alaskan	LCDR E. P. Ferry
Hawaiian	
Philippine	————
<u>Naval Districts</u>	
1st	CDR Robert Woodbury
	LCDR Garceau
3rd	LT P. S. Smith
4th	CDR E. S. McCawley
5th	CDR C. A. Russell
6th	LT E. A. Hummel
7th	LT J. A. Reynolds
8th	LT M. F. Nelson
9th	LT E. S. Meany
10th	LT J. A. O'Connor
11th	LT C. C. Cumberland
12th	LCDR C. E. Odegaard
13th	LT W. G. Jordon

14th
15th   LT Leo J. Roland
16th   ———
17th   ———

Major Commands

   South Pacific   LT John Burke
                               LT James A. Michener

   3rd Fleet
   5th Fleet   ———
   7th Fleet   ———
   8th Fleet   CDR J. M. Boit
                               LCDR Carl Bridenbaugh
   9th Fleet   LCDR E. P. Ferry
                               LT Ernest Leet
   10th Fleet
   12th Fleet   LCDR P. G. Van der Poel

Shore Establishments

   Naval Gun Factory   LT C. E. Nowell
   Washington Navy Yard   LT C. E. Nowell
   Potomac River Naval   LT C. E. Nowell
    Command
   Severn River Naval
    Command   ———
   Naval Torpedo Station,   Mr. R. Powell
    Newport
   Naval War College   ———
   NOB Iceland   LT P. T. Sprinz
   NOB Trinidad   LCDR R. F. Millett
   NOB Guantanamo   LCDR Lambert

United States Marine Corps   COL John Potts
                                              CAPT W. G. Wendell
                                              CAPT P. D. Carleton
                                              CAPT C. P. Morehouse
                                              CAPT W. H. Goodman

INDEX

Note: This index refers to entry numbers, rather than page numbers.

A

ABDA; See American, British, Dutch, Australian Area Command

Academy, United States Naval, Annapolis, Maryland, 33, 136, 137

Accounting, 3, 39, 90, 91, 93, 95, 97, 129; See also Finance

Accounting Group, Bureau of Supplies and Accounts, 90

Accounting and Statistical Section, Bureau of Supplies and Accounts, 97

Adak, Alaska, 108, 156

Administration Section, Bureau of Supplies and Accounts, 97

Administrative Command, Amphibious Forces, U. S. Pacific Fleet, Marianas, 150

Administrative Command, Commander Minecraft Pacific Fleet, 153

Administrative Planning Division, Bureau of Supplies and Accounts, 101

Administrative Services, Bureau of Naval Personnel, 86

Advanced Base Section, Bureau of Supplies and Accounts, 101

Advanced Base Section, Oahu, Hawaii, 155

Aerology, 62, 140, 150, 156, 157, 163

Aeronautics, Bureau of, 8, 28, 37, 38, 46-67, 91

Africa, 148

Air Bases, Naval, Eighth Naval District, 115

Aircraft Procurement Act of 1926, 37

Air Force, Atlantic Fleet, 142

Air Material Center, Naval, Philadelphia, Pennsylvania, 111

Air-Sea Rescue, 109, 113, 158

Airships; See Lighter-than-Air Craft

Air Stations, Marine

    El Centro, California, 118

    El Toro, California, 118

    Miramar, California, 118

    Mojave, California, 118

    Santa Barbara, California, 118

Air Stations, Naval

    Atlantic City, New Jersey, 111

    Cape May, New Jersey, 111

    Guantanamo, Cuba, 165

    Hampton Roads, Virginia, 33

    Lakehurst, New Jersey, 111

    New Cumberland, Pennsylvania, 111

    Patuxent River, Maryland, 126

    Pensacola, Florida, 33

    Quonset Point, Rhode Island, 32

    San Diego, California, 33, 118

    Wildwood, New Jersey, 111

    Willow Grove, Pennsylvania, 111

Air Support Control Units, Commander, 150

Air Test Center, Patuxent River, Maryland, 127

Air Training Command, Naval, Pensacola, Florida, 34

Air Transportation Service, Naval, 29, 107

Alaska, 120, 156, 170

Alaskan Sea Frontier, 156

Alaskan Sector, Thirteenth Naval District, 156

Albion, Robert G., Dr., App. A

Aleutian Islands Campaign, 68

Alger, Mark W., Lieutenant, App. A

All Forces, Aruba-Curacao, Commander, 164

<u>All Hands</u> (Magazine), 85

Allied Commission, Austria, 147

Allied Expeditionary Force, 25

Allied Forces, Commander in Chief, 148

Allied Missions

    Low Countries, 147

Scandinavia, 147

Allied Tanker Coordinating Committee, 13

Allies, 25, 32, 76, 109, 159, 162, 168; See also Specific Country

    Occupation, 23

    Shipping, 109, 120, 146, 160

Aluminum, 4

Amapa, Brazil, 146

Amchitka, Alaska, 156

American, British, Dutch, Australian Area (ABDA) Command, 159

Ammunition, 76, 131, 148; See also Ordnance

Ammunition Depots, Naval, 115, 168

    Crane, Indiana, 127

    Fall Brook, California, 127

    Fort Mifflin, Pennsylvania, 111

    Hawthorne, Nevada, 127

    Hingham, Massachusetts, 109

    McAlister, Oklahoma, 127

    St. Julien's Creek, Virginia, 127

Ammunition Quality Evaluation Unit, Bureau of Ordnance, 73

Amphibious Forces

    U. S. Atlantic Fleet, 145

    U. S. Pacific Fleet, 150

Amphibious Ships and Craft, 20, 150

Amphibious Training Command, U. S. Atlantic Fleet, 145

Amphibious Warfare, 68, 138, 145, 150, 153, 159

Andrews, George A., Lieutenant Commander, App. A

Annapolis, Maryland, 33, 136, 137

Anne Arundel County, Maryland, 136

Anti-Aircraft School, Pacific Beach, California, 152

Anti-Aircraft Weapons, 75, 79; See also Ordnance

Antigua, British West Indies, 160

Antisubmarine Warfare, 113, 138, 139, 141, 142, 146, 160-162, 165-167, 172, 173

   Commands, 10, 11

   Training, 143, 151, 152

   Weapons, 78, 131, 132, 143

ANZAC; See Australia-New Zealand Area Command

Appropriations, 30, 37, 60, 74, 81, 123; See also Legislation

Appropriations Committee, 30; See also Congress

Area Petroleum Office, Oahu, Hawaii, 155

Argentia, Newfoundland, 109, 139

Arizona, 118, 169

Arkansas, 127

Armed Guard, 110, 164, 172, 173

Armed Guard Center, Naval, Third Naval District, 110

Armed Guard Service, Naval, 172, 173

Armor, 51, 76; See also Ordnance

Army, 113, 120, 157, 160

Army Air Force, 54

Army-Navy Munitions Board, 22

Army-Navy Petroleum Board, 13; See also Petroleum

Army-Navy Relations, 63, 88, 107, 113, 120, 122, 145, 149, 156, 159, 161

    Aviation, 28, 54

    Installations, 140, 168

    Ordnance, 20, 70, 76

    Planning, 166

    Procurement, 13, 38, 102

Army Provost Marshal, 14

Aruba-Curacao, 160, 164

Arvidson, Florence E., Ensign, App. A

Asheville, North Carolina, 113

Askew, William C., Lieutenant (junior grade), 20, 173

Assistant Chief of Naval Operations (Material), 17

Assistant Commandant (Operations), Third Naval District, 110

Assistant District Security Officer, Baltimore, Maryland, 112

Astronomy; See Observatory, Naval

Athletics; See Physical Fitness

Atlantic Campaign, 138-148

Atlantic City, New Jersey, 111

Atlantic Fleet, 45, 138-148

Atlantic Squadron, 138

Atomic Bomb, 89

Attache, Naval, London, England, 147

Attu, 156

Australia-New Zealand Area Command, 159

Austria, 147

Aviation, 16, 27-45, 47-67, 119, 134, 142, 157-159, 163, 168

    Facilities, 16, 32, 33, 58, 108, 111, 115, 118, 126, 156, 165-167, 169

    Finance, 60

    Maintenance and Repair, 55, 73, 133, 142

    Marine Corps, 32, 46, 67, 118

    Ordnance, 38, 51, 73, 76, 79, 132, 142

    Personnel, 31, 40, 41, 53, 59, 87

    Planning, 30, 31, 52

    Procurement and Production, 29, 31, 37, 39, 51-54, 79, 91

    Research and Development, 57, 73, 126

    Training, 29, 33-35, 48, 61, 67, 126, 152

"Aviation Shore Establishments, 1911-1945," 58

Aviation Supply Annex, Oakland, California, 133

Aviation Supply Division, Bureau of Supplies and Accounts, 91

Aviation Supply Liaison Division, Bureau of Supplies and Accounts, 91

Aviation Supply Office, Bureau of Supplies and Accounts, 56

Aviation Supply Office, Bureau of Supplies and Accounts, Philadelphia, Pennsylvania, 91

Awards, Medals, and Citations, 82, 149, 170

Axis, 64, 140, 142, 146; See also Individual Countries, Enemy Documents and Equipment

B

Bahia, Brazil, 146

Bainbridge, Maryland, 112

Balboa, Panama, 122

Ballantine, Duncan S., Lieutenant, 18, 20, 21, App. A

Baltimore, Maryland, 112

Barber Shops, 105

Barracks, Naval

    Treasure Island, California, 119

    Washington, D.C., 135

Base Force, U. S. Pacific Fleet, 155

Base Maintenance Division, 15, 21; See also Bases and Shore Activities

Base, Naval, Puerto Castilla, Honduras, 122

Bases and Shore Activities, 1, 21, 101, 109, 111, 112, 115, 120, 133, 140, 169; See also Individual Bases

    Advanced Bases, 21, 108, 115, 122, 133, 139, 140, 146-148, 154, 156, 158, 160, 162, 168, 170

    Air Bases, 32, 58, 111, 122, 126, 140, 160, 166-168

    Maintenance, 14, 15, 21

Bath, Maine, 109

Beers, Henry, Specialist Second Class, 80

Belem, Brazil, 146

Belgium, 147

Bennett, Harrison L., 171

Berger, Carl, 47, 55-57

Bergmark, D. A., Lieutenant, 38

Berkeley, California, 125

Berkeley, Francis L., Jr., Lieutenant, 173

Bermuda, 167

Bikini Atomic Tests, 89

Black Personnel, 83, 84, 115, 127

Blimps; See Lighter-than-Air Craft

Blum, J., Lieutenant, 18

Boit, Julian M., Commander, 148, App. A

Bolander, Louis H., 136

Bombs, 76, 79; See also Ordnance

Bonds; See War Bonds

Booz, Fry, Allen, and Hamilton, 49, 80, 91

Boston, Massachusetts, 109

Boston Navy Yard, 109

Brazil, 146

Brewington, Marion V., Lieutenant Commander, 164

Bridenbaugh, Carl, Lieutenant Commander, 148, App. A

Britain; See Great Britain

British Guiana, 166

British Home Fleet, 138

British - U. S. Relations, 13, 25, 121, 134, 138, 139, 147, 164, 166, 167; See also U. S. - Allied Relations

British West Indies, 160, 162, 166

Bronx, New York, 88

Brown, Nettie T., Ensign, 111

Brown, Robert Vance, Lieutenant (junior grade), 39

Bruske, Paul W., Lieutenant, 100

Buchanan, Albert R., Lieutenant, 38, App. A

Buddeke, John W., Lieutenant (junior grade), 122

Budget Division, Bureau of Supplies and Accounts, 96

<u>Building the Navy's Bases in World War II</u>, 108

Bureau of Aeronautics; See Aeronautics, Bureau of

Bureau of Medicine and Surgery; See Medicine and Surgery, Bureau of

Bureau of Naval Personnel; See Personnel, Bureau of Naval

Bureau of Ordnance; See Ordnance, Bureau of

Bureau of Ships; See Ships, Bureau of

Bureau of Supplies and Accounts; See Supplies and Accounts, Bureau of

Bureau of Yards and Docks; See Yards and Docks, Bureau of

Bureaus, 20, 23, 25, 27, 70; See also Individual Bureaus

Burke, John, Lieutenant, App. A

C

California

    Northern Naval Activities, 119, 125, 132, 133, 163

    Southern Naval Activities, 33, 118, 127, 132, 150, 152, 169

California Institute of Technology, 132

Camp Lejeune, North Carolina, 46

Camp Parks, California, 119

Camp Peary, Virginia, 112

Camp Pendleton, California, 118

Camp Pendleton Boat Basin, California, 118

Canada, 120, 139

Canal Zone; See Panama

Canton, Ohio, 128

Cape May, New Jersey, 111

Carbon, 2

Caribbean, 117; See also Specific Countries

Caribbean Naval Coastal Frontier, 160

Caribbean Sea Frontier, 160, 165, 166

Carleton, P. D., Captain, App. A

Carney, Robert B., Captain, 140

Caroline Islands Campaign, 68

Carrigan, Richard M., Lieutenant Commander, 40

Cary, Peter, Lieutenant, App. A

Casualties, 68, 69, 85

Cedar Falls, Iowa, 88

Censorship, 121, 149

Centerline, Michigan, 128

Central America, 122; See also Individual Countries

Chambers, Moreau B., Lieutenant Commander, 34

Chapel Hill, North Carolina, 113

Chaplains' Corps, 86, 109, 147, 155, 157

The Chaplain's Newsletter, 86

Charleston, South Carolina, 113

Charleston Navy Yard, South Carolina, 113

Charlic, Carl, 57

Charlotte, North Carolina, 127

Chase, Theodore, Lieutenant Commander, 5

Chemical Warfare, 119

Chemical Warfare Training Unit, Navy, Dugway Proving Ground, Utah, 119

Chemistry, 134

Chesapeake Bay, 112

Chicago, Illinois, 82

Chief Clerk's Division, Bureau of Supplies and Accounts, 99

Chief of Naval Operations, Office of, 11-45, 123-126

China Lake, California; See Inyokern, California

Chinese Language, 125

Citations; See Awards, Medals, and Citations

Civil Aeronautics Administration, 35

Civil Affairs, 23, 157; See also Military Government

Civil Engineer Corps, 108

Civil Engineer Corps Officer Training School, Davisville, Rhode Island, 109

Civilian Personnel, 1, 74, 90, 99, 118, 133, 167, 169; See also Personnel

    Offices and Units, 109, 119-121

    Training, 1, 59

Clark County, Nevada, 118

Cleveland, Ohio, 90

Clothing, 92, 102

Clothing Division, Bureau of Supplies and Accounts, 92

Coast Guard, 141, 157, 160

Coast Guard Anti-Submarine Flotilla, 162

Coast Guard-Navy Relations, 3, 140

Coastal Patrol, 113, 140, 165

Cocoanut Grove, Boston, Disaster, 109

Coco Solo, Panama, 122

College Entrance Examination Board, 83

College Training Section, Bureau of Naval Personnel, 83

Collins, James F., Lieutenant, 121

Collins, John W., Lieutenant Commander, 119

Colorado, 119, 125

Columbia, South Carolina, 113

Columbia University, 23

Colvin, James E., Lieutenant, 102, App. A

Combat Information Center, 151

Combat Information Center Indoctrination School, San Diego, California, 152

Combat and Operational Intelligence Branch, Sixth Naval District, 113

Commerce Section, Transportation Division, Bureau of Supplies and Accounts, 107

Commissary Stores, 104

Committee for Standardization of Terminology for Activities of the Navy, 116

Committee to Study Command Relationships in Naval Districts, 116

Communications, 11, 16, 49, 149, 170; See also Radio Service, Naval

    Offices and Units, 111, 114-116, 119, 121, 122, 144, 147, 148, 157, 162, 163, 165, 166

    Procedures, 110, 142, 151

    Radio, 87, 134, 140

    Training, 109, 129

Communications, Division of Naval, 16

Communications Office, First Naval District, 109

Compasses, 51

Congress, U. S., 30, 37, 48, 57, 101

Connecticut, 109, 110, 170

Connery, Robert H., Lieutenant Commander, 164, App. A

Construction

    Advanced Base, 108, 157, 162, 164, 165, 167, 168

    Continental U. S., 106, 108, 118, 128, 137

Construction Battalions, 108

Containers Division, Office of Procurement and Material, 98

Contracting, 2-7, 81, 108, 136

    Aviation, 38, 39, 53

    Negotiation, Renegotiation, Termination, 7, 93, 103, 104

    Offices and Units, 7, 81, 93

    Ordnance, 72, 73, 79

    Policy, 38, 53

Control Council, Germany, 147

Convoys, 11, 109, 165; See also Merchant Shipping

    Activities and Units, 11, 110, 121

    Defense, 11, 112, 113, 138, 139, 146, 163, 164

Coordinator of Research and Development, Office of, 8, 9, 25; See also Research and Development

Copper, 2, 4

Corona, California, 169

Coronado, California, 150

Corrective Services Division, Bureau of Naval Personnel, 85

Corsica, 148

Cost Inspection Service, Bureau of Supplies and Accounts, 93

Counsel, Office of, Bureau of Ordnance, 74; See also Legal Matters

Craig, John, Captain, 1

Crane, Indiana, 127

Crossroads Operation, 89

Cruisers, 151

Cuba, 160, 162, 165

Cumberland, Charles C., Lieutenant, 118, App. A

Curacao, 164

Cushman, Frank, Commander, 1

D

Dahlgren, Virginia, 132

Dartmouth College, 83

Dater, Henry M., Lieutenant Commander, 43, App. A

Davis, Ashley F., 48, 58, 63

Davisville, Rhode Island, 109

Decorations; See Awards, Medals, and Citations

Defense Aid Material Movement Section, Transportation Division, Bureau of Supplies and Accounts, 107

Defense Aid Section, Bureau of Supplies and Accounts, 96

Delaware, 111

Denmark, 140

Dependents Welfare Division, Bureau of Naval Personnel, 85

Depth Charges, 78, 131; See also Ordnance

Deputy Chief of Naval Operations (Air), 27-45, 56, 58

    Organizational Changes, 49, 50, 52, 59, 62, 66

Design Unit, Bureau of Ordnance, 73

Design Unit, Bureau of Ordnance, Pasadena, California, 132

Destroyers, 141, 151, 153

Destroyers, Atlantic Fleet, 141

Destroyers/Cruisers, Pacific Fleet, 151

Destroyer Escorts, 141

Director of Enlisted Personnel, Bureau of Naval Personnel, 87

Director of Naval Reserve, Ninth Naval District, 116

Director of Women's Reserve, Bureau of Naval Personnel, 88

Director of Women's Reserve, Sixth Naval District, 113

Disbursing Division, Bureau of Supplies and Accounts, 90

Disciplinary Barracks, Shoemaker, California, 119

Disciplinary Matters, 85, 87, 88, 119, 122, 155, 169

District Intelligence Office, First Naval District, 109

District Operations Office, First Naval District, 109

District Planning and Coordinating Office, Third Naval District, 110

District Property Transportation Offices, 107

Districts, Naval, 109-122; See also Specific District

Dodds, R. H., Lieutenant, App. A

Drury, Alfred T., 134

Drydocks, 108

Drydocks, Naval, NOB Terminal Island, California, 169

Dugway Proving Ground, Utah, 119

Dutch Harbor, Alaska, 156, 170

Dutch-U. S. Relations, 160, 164

Dutton, Granville W., 61, 65, 66

DuVon, Jay, Lieutenant, 45

E

Eastern Sea Frontier, 109, 111, 113, 161

Eckernforde, Germany, 130

Education; See Training

Ehrman, Kent S., Lieutenant, 111

Eighth Fleet, 148

Eighth Naval District, 115, 162

Ekdahl, Kenneth J., Lieutenant, 144, App. A

El Centro, California, 118

Electronics, 4, 17, 134; See also Specific Equipment

Electronics Section, Office of the Chief of Naval Operations, 17

Eleventh Naval District, 46, 118, 163, 169

Elk Hills, California, 169

Ellice Island, 158

El Toro, California, 118

Enemy Documents and Equipment, 25

Engineering, Bureau of, 134

Engineering Experiment Station, Severn River Naval Command, 136

England; See Great Britain

Eniwetok, 157

Ennis, Meta A., Lieutenant (junior grade), App. A

Equipment; See Material

Escort Carrier Pre-Commissioning School, Puget Sound Navy Yard, Washington, 152

Europe, 32, 45, 68, 108, 138, 147; See also Individual Countries

Executive Order No. 9112, 5

Experimental Model Basin, Washington Navy Yard, Washington, D.C., 129

F

Fairbanks, H. R., Lieutenant, App. A

Fallbrook, California, 118, 127

Farber Committee; See Committee to Study Command Relationships in Naval Districts

Farfan, Panama, 122

Federal Bureau of Investigation, 14

Fennemore, George M., Lieutenant (junior grade), 33, 34

Ferry, E. P., Lieutenant Commander, App. A

Field Administration Division, Bureau of Naval Personnel, 83, 88

Field Branch Liaison Division, Bureau of Supplies and Accounts, 90

Field Operations Branch, Bureau of Supplies and Accounts, 98

Fifteenth Naval District, 46, 122

Fifth Naval District, 112

Finance, 5, 30, 60, 71, 74, 90, 93, 108, 130; See also Accounting, Contracting

    Appropriations, 30, 60, 80, 96

    Cost Inspection, 93, 109

    Offices and Units, 5, 80, 81, 93, 144

    Planning, 30, 60

Finance Division, Office of Procurement and Material, 5

Finance and Material Division, Bureau of Naval Personnel, 81

Financial Division, Bureau of Ordnance, 74

Fire Control, 79, 128; See also Ordnance

Firefighters School, Naval, NOB Terminal Island, California, 169

First Naval District, 109

Fishery Rights, 121

Fleet Air Wings, 44; See also Individual Fleet Air Wings

Fleet Air Wings

    One, Three, Four, Fourteen, Sixteen, Seventeen, 44

Fleet Exercises, 36

Fleet Maintenance Section, Office of the Chief of Naval Operations, 17, 20

Fleet Marine Force, Pacific, 46

Fleet Operational Training Command, 143, 152

Fleets

    Atlantic, 45, 138-148

    Eighth, 148

    Fourth, 146

    Pacific, 149-159

    Seventh, 159

    Tenth, 10, 11

    United States, 10-12, 45

Fleet Training Center, Oahu, Hawaii, 155

Florida, 33, 34, 113, 114, 162, 171

Food, 102, 104; See also Subsistence Division, Bureau of Supplies and Accounts

Forces, Naval

    Azores, 147

    Europe, 147

    Germany, 147

    Mediterranean, 147

    Northern Solomons, 154

    Northwest African Waters, 148

    Southwest Pacific, 159

Ford, Mary Louise, Lieutenant, 126

Foreign Aid, 64, 97; See also Lend-Lease

Forester, Donald M., Lieutenant, 32

Forest Park, Illinois, 128

Fort Mifflin, Pennsylvania, 111

Fort Story, Virginia, 112

Fortaleza, Brazil, 146

Forward Area, Central Pacific, Commander, 158

Forward Area Representatives, 151

Fourteenth Naval District, 121

Fourth Fleet, 146

Fourth Naval District, 111

France, 68, 108, 147, 148, 160

Francis, Dennis L., Captain, 111

French Antilles, 160

Fuel, 94, 102, 154; See also Petroleum, Tankers

    Storage, 94, 108, 133, 164, 169

    Transportation, 24, 94, 133, 164

Fuel Annexes, Naval

    Elk Hills, California, 169

    Terminal Island, California, 169

Fuel Depot, Navy, Point Molate, California, 133

Fuel Division, Bureau of Supplies and Accounts, 94

Fuel and Transportation Division, Bureau of Supplies and Accounts, 106

Furer, Julius A., Rear Admiral, 8, 9

Fuzes, 76, 128, 131; See also Ordnance

G

Galapagos Islands, 108

Gare Loch, Scotland, 139

Gatun, Panama, 122

Geen, Elizabeth, Lieutenant, 88

General Purchase Division, Bureau of Supplies and Accounts, 103

General Stock Division, Bureau of Supplies and Accounts, 98

George, James C., Lieutenant, 1

Georgia, 113

Germany, 25, 112, 130, 138, 147

    U-Boats, 138-142, 146, 160, 162, 167

Gilbert Islands, 158

Gilberts Campaign, 43, 68, 157

Gilmore, Myron P., Lieutenant, 18, App. A

Gleason, John H., Lieutenant, 21, App. A

Gliders, 39; See also Aviation

Golden, Rose L., Lieutenant, 42, 43

Goodman, W. H., Captain, App. A

Grady Report, 90

Graham, Donald S., Lieutenant Commander, 170

Graves, T. J., Ensign, App. A

Graves, V. R., Ensign, App. A

Great Britian, 13, 139, 140, 147, 160, 164, 170;
    See also British - U. S. Relations

Great Lakes, Illinois, 83, 116

Greenland, 45, 138, 140

Greenland Patrol, 140

Guam, 149

Guantanamo, Cuba, 160, 165

Guantanamo Sector, Caribbean Sea Frontier, 165

Gulf Sea Frontier, 114, 162

Gulf States, 115

Gun Factory, Naval, Washington, D.C., 128, 129

Guns; See Ordnance

Guthrie, Chester L., Lieutenant Commander, 68, 69
    App. A

H

Haiti, 165

Halifax, Nova Scotia, 139

Hampton Roads, Virginia, 33

Harbor Defense, 109, 112, 155, 164-166

    Net and Boom Defenses, 78, 113, 132, 143

Harbor Entrance Control Posts
- Fort Story, Virginia, 112
- New York Harbor, 110

Harford, L. W., 13

Harvard University, 125

Hawaii, 68, 121, 149, 155, 170

Hawaiian Sea Frontier, 43, 121

Hawthorne, Nevada, 127

Hayden, Sherman, Lieutenant, 82, App. A

Hazzard, William H., Commander, 170

Heicher, Winchester H., Lieutenant (junior grade), App. A

Hellweg, J. F., Commodore, 124

Herring, Frank W., Lieutenant Commander, App. A

Herring, Louise, 8

Hilen, Andrew R., Jr., Lieutenant, 42, App. A

Hingham, Massachusetts, 109, 127

Historical Programs, 101

<u>History of the Medical Department of the United States Navy in World War II</u>, 68, 69

History, Office of Naval, 47, 101; See also Records and Library, Office of

<u>History of United States Naval Aviation</u>, 28

Hockenbury, Myron D., Lieutenant, 111

Honduras, 122

Hospital, Naval, Severn River Naval Command, 136

Household Effects Section, Transportation Division, Bureau of Supplies and Accounts, 107

House Naval Affairs Committee, 30; See also Congress

Howe, Daniel R., Lieutenant, 1

Hubbard, R. D., Lieutenant, App. A

Hummel, Edward A., Lieutenant, 113, App. A

Hurst, J. W., Lieutenant, App. A

Hurst, Willard, Lieutenant, 81, 82

Hydrographic Office, 123

Hydrography, 121, 123, 147, 155

I

Iceland, 45, 168

Idaho, 120, 128

Illinois, 82, 83, 116, 128

Indian Head, Maryland, 132

Indiana, 88, 127, 128

Indianapolis, Indiana, 128

Industrial Mananger, Eighth Naval District, 115

Industrial Mobilization, 2, 70, 111, 113, 116, 128, 163

    Aircraft Procurement and Production, 37, 38, 48

    Finance, 5, 37, 38, 103

    Procurement and Production, 2, 5, 6, 22, 37, 38, 89, 94, 103

    Raw Materials, 2, 22, 103

Informational Services Section, Bureau of Naval Personnel, 85

Inspection Division, Office of Procurement and Material, 38

Inspections, 12, 54, 72, 83, 92, 93, 104, 109

Inspector General of the Army, 12

Inspector General, Office of the Naval, 10, 12

Integrated Aeronautic Program, 49

<u>The Integration of the Negro into the U. S. Navy</u>, 84

Intelligence, 26, 66, 151, 159

    Offices and Activities, 109, 113-116, 119-121, 130, 136, 147, 148, 157, 163, 166

    Photographic, 61, 66, 149

Intelligence, Office of Naval, 14, 23, 26, 125

International Aid Division, Bureau of Supplies and Accounts, 96, 97

Inter-Service Relations, 110, 111, 115, 134, 149, 165; See also Joint, Individual Services

    Supply, 94, 104

Inyokern, California, 118, 132

Iowa, 88

Island Governments, Office of, 23; See also Military Government

Italy, 148

Iwo Jima, 108, 158

Iwo Jima Campaign, 42, 68

J

Jackson, Donald, Lieutenant (junior grade), 8

Jamaica, 165

James, E. T., Lieutenant, App. A

Japan, 68, 78, 156

Japanese Language, 125

Jarchow, Merrill E., Liuetenant, 42

Java, 170

Johnson Atoll, 121

Johnson Dudley, Lieutenant, 83

Johnson, E. D. H., Lieutenant, App. A

Joint, 122, 153, 156, 157; See also Army-Navy Relations, Individual Services

Joint Operations Center, Sixth Naval District, 113

Jones, W. T., Lieutenant, App. A

Jordan, W. G., Lieutenant, App. A

July, Robert W., Lieutenant, 43

Juneau, Alaska, 156

K

Kearney, Marguerite A., 92

Keller, Donald, Commander, 111

Kelley, John J., Lieutenant, 111

Kemble, John H., Lieutenant Commander, App. A

Kemler, E. J., Lieutenant, App. A

King, John P., Lieutenant, 45

Kiska, 156

Klapp, O. E., Lieutenant (junior grade), App. A

Klein, Philip S., Lieutenant Commander, 163, App. A

Kodiak, Alaska, 156

Koldewey Island, 140

Kurile Islands Campaign, 156

Kwajalein, 157

L

La Barre, Winston, Lieutenant, App. A

Labor Relations, 109, 118; See also Personnel

Lakehurst, New Jersey, 111

Lambert, Lieutenant Commander, App. A

Land, William G., Lieutenant (junior grade), App. A

Landing Craft, 138, 145, 150, 159

Landwehr, Clifton E., Lieutenant (junior grade), 111

Language Training, 125

Langworthy, D. M. S., Lieutenant Colonel (British), 13

Laundries, 105

Leet, Ernest, Lieutenant, App. A

Legal Matters, 37, 124

    Offices and Units, 74, 81, 116, 119, 121, 157, 169

Legislation, 7, 30, 88; See also Appropriations, Congress

Le Havre, France, 108

Lend-Lease, 19, 92, 133, 147; See also U. S.-Allied Relations

    Aviation Aid, 38, 64

    Finance and Accounting, 74, 90, 96, 97

    Ordnance, 71, 74

Lewis, James A., Captain, 109

Life Insurance, 85

Lighter-than-Air Craft, 37, 111, 118, 146

Lindley, A. D., Lieutenant Commander, App. A

Litchfield Park, Arizona, 169

Livingston, Craig A., Lieutenant, 145, App. A

Local Defense, 122, 157, 158, 165, 168, 169; See also Harbor Defense

    Planning, 110, 135, 166

    Units, 109, 112, 119, 121

Local Defense Force, Naval, 109

Logistics Office, First Naval District, 109

Logistics Planning, 17, 18, 21, 24, 101; See also Supply, Material, Construction

Logistics Planning Division, Bureau of Supplies and Accounts, 101

Logistics Planning Unit, Office of the Chief of Naval Operations, 18; See also Logistics Planning

London, England, 13, 147

Londonderry, Northern Ireland, 139

Long, Clarence D., Lieutenant, App. A

Long Beach, California, 169

Loomis, Alfred F., Captain, 13

Lord, Charlotte V., Lieutenant (junior grade), 111

Lord, Clifford L., Lieutenant Commander, 28, 33, App. A

Los Alamitos, California, 169

Louisiana, 85, 115, 171

Luce, Gardiner, Commander, 111

Lumber, 102

Lunny, Robert M., Lieutenant Commander, 151

Luxembourg, 147

M

MacArthur, Douglas, General, 159

Magazine, Naval, Port Chicago, California, 127

Mahan, Alfred Thayer, Rear Admiral, 18

Mail Service; See Postal Service

Maine, 109

Maine Maritime Academy, 109

Maintenance, 49, 55, 73, 78, 92, 112, 142; See also Shipbuilding and Repair

    Offices and Units, 14-17, 73

    Ships and Craft, 20, 89, 145, 150, 163

Maintenance Division, Bureau of Ordnance, 73

Maintenance Division, Bureau of Supplies and Accounts, 96

Majuro, 157

Malay Language, 125

Manpower; See Personnel

Manpower Survey Committee, 116

Mariana Islands, 150, 158

Mariana Islands Campaign, 68

Marianas Area, Commander, 158

Marine Corps, 46, 69, 113, 119, 157

    Aviation, 32, 34, 67, 118

Marine Corps Base, Guantanamo, Cuba, 165

Marine Corps-Navy Relations, 3, 145

Marine Corps, Office of the Commandant, U. S., 46

Marine Corps Women's Reserve, 46

Marion, John, Lieutenant, App. A

Maritime Commission, 14; See also Merchant Shipping

Markham, George H., Lieutenant, App. A

Markoff, George P., Commander, 11

Marshall Islands, 43, 157, 158

Marshalls Campaign, 68, 157

Marshalls-Gilberts Area, Commander, 157

Marvin, George, App. A

Maryland, 33, 109, 112, 126, 127, 132, 135-137

Massachusetts, 88, 109, 127

Massachusetts Maritime Academy, 109

Materials, 25, 71-73, 79; See also Industrial Mobilization, Procurement, Production, Supply

    Allocation, 4, 22, 81, 91, 97, 163

    Aviation, 51, 54, 56, 91, 157

    Offices and Units, 2-4, 22, 81, 98, 157

    Procurement, 2-4, 22, 69, 91, 102, 103, 130, 163

    Raw Materials, 2-4, 22, 103

    Supply, 56, 73, 98

Materials Division, Office of the Chief of Naval Operations, 22

Mathews, Joseph J., Lieutenant, App. A

Mattisen, P. M., Lieutenant Commander, 93

McAlister, Oklahoma, 127

McCarthy, Francis X., Lieutenant, 114

McCawley, E. S., Commander, App. A

McKenna, Bernard, Lieutenant, 13

McLean, J. E., Lieutenant (junior grade), App. A

Meany, E. S., Lieutenant, App. A

Medals; See Awards, Medals, and Citations

Medical Services, 65, 68, 69, 108, 109, 111, 170

    Activities and Units, 114, 116, 119, 121, 129, 130, 144, 157, 165, 166

Medicine and Surgery, Bureau of, 68, 69, 85

Mediterranean Sea, 147, 148

Melville, Rhode Island, 171

Merchant Shipping, 24, 107; See also Convoys, Tankers, Armed Guard

    Allied, 120, 160, 162

    Defense, 11, 110, 112, 120, 121, 146, 162-164, 172

Metallurgy, 62, 134

Meteorology; See Aerology

Mexico, 163

Miami, Florida, 114, 162, 171

Michener, James A., Lieutenant, App. A

Michigan, 128

Midshipmen's School (WR), Northampton, Massachusetts, 88

Midway, 121

Military Government, 23, 101, 149, 157, 158; See also Civil Affairs, Island Governments, Office of

Miller, Taulman A., Lieutenant, 40, 41

Millett, Robert F., Lieutenant Commander, 166, App. A

Minecraft, Battle Force, 153

Minecraft, Pacific Fleet, 153

Mine Depot, Naval, Yorktown, Virginia, 132

Mine Laboratory, Bureau of Ordnance, 131

Mine Warfare, 15, 78, 113, 129, 131, 153

    Minesweeping, 109, 112, 143, 153

    Ordnance, 15, 76, 78, 129, 131, 132

    Research and Development, 15, 131, 132

Mine Warfare Test Station, Naval, Solomons, Maryland, 132

Ministry of Fuel and Power (British), 13

Miramar, California, 118

Mitchell, Billy, General, 28

Mobile Display Unit, 92

Model Basin, 129

Mojave, California, 118

Molate, California, 133

Montana, 120

Morale, 121, 170

Morehouse, C. P., Captain, App. A

Morison, Elting E., Lieutenant, App. A

Morrow Board, 28

Motor Torpedo Boat, 154, 171

Motor Torpedo Boat Commissioning Details, New Orleans, Louisiana, New York, New York, 171

Motor Torpedo Boat Shakedown Detail, Miami, Florida, 171

Motor Torpedo Boat Squadrons, South Pacific Area, 154

Motor Torpedo Boat Squadrons Training Center, Melville, Rhode Island, 171

Motor Transport Section, Transportation Division, Bureau of Supplies and Accounts, 107

<u>N</u>

Natal, Brazil, 146

National Defense Research Committee, 83, 134

National Service Life Insurance, 85

Naval Districts, 109-122; See also Individual Districts

Naval Research Laboratory; See Research Laboratory, Naval

Navigation, 123, 124

<u>Navy Register</u>, 82

Navy Relief Society, 109, 121

"Navy Shipment Marking Handbook," 107

Navy Yards, 108, 129; See also Individual Navy Yards

Negro Personnel; See Black Personnel

Nelson, Dennis D., 84

Nelson, M. F., Lieutenant, App. A

Net Depots, Naval

    Guantanamo, Cuba, 165

    Newport, Rhode Island, 109

Terminal Island, California, 169

Tiburon, California, 132

Netherlands, 147; See also Dutch-U. S. Relations

Netherlands East Indies, 68

Netherlands West Indies, 160, 164

Neutrality Patrol, 146

Nevada, 119, 127

New Cumberland, Pennsylvania, 111

Newell, Thomas N., Lieutenant, 151

New England, 109

Newfoundland, 45, 109, 139

New Guinea Campaign, 68

New Hampshire, 109

New Jersey, 109-111

New London, Connecticut, 170

New Mexico, 118

New Orleans, Louisiana, 82, 115, 171

Newport, Rhode Island, 109, 130

New York, 88, 109, 110, 161, 171

New York, New York, 109, 110, 161, 171

New Zealand, 159

Ninth Naval District, 116

Norfolk, Virginia, 112, 142-144

Normandy Invasion, 68, 138, 140, 147

North African Invasion, 68, 138, 145

Northampton, Massachusetts, 88, 109

North Atlantic Naval Coastal Frontier, 161

North Carolina, 46, 112, 113, 127

Northeast Greenland Patrol, 140

Northern Group, Eastern Sea Frontier, 109

North Pacific Area, 156

North Pacific Force and Area, 156

Northwest Sea Frontier, 120, 156

Nowell, C. E., Lieutenant, App. A

Nuclear Warfare, 89

O

Oahu, Hawaii, 121, 155

Oakland, California, 133

Observatory, Naval, 124

Occupied Areas Section, Office of the Chief of Naval Operations, 23

Ocker, Margaret, Lieutenant, 102, 103

O'Connor, J. A., Lieutenant, App. A

Odegaard, C. E., Lieutenant Commander, 119, App. A

Office of the Chief of Naval Operations; See Chief of Naval Operations, Office of the

Office of Naval Intelligence; See Intelligence, Office of Naval

Office of Research and Inventions; See Research and Inventions, Office of

Officer Procurement Division, Bureau of Naval Personnel, 82

Officer Procurement Division, Bureau of Supplies and Accounts, 99

Officers' Accounts Division, 90

Ohio, 90, 128

Okinawa Campaign, 42, 68, 108

Oklahoma, 88, 127

Operating Bases, Naval

    Balboa, Panama, 122

    Bermuda, 167

    Guantanamo Bay, Cuba, 165

    Iceland, 168

    Norfolk, Virginia, 112

    Terminal Island, California, 169

    Trinidad, British West Indies, 166

Operations Research Group, Gulf Sea Frontier, 162

Optics, 134

Ordnance, 70-79, 127-132; See also Specific Weapons and Equipment

    Facilities, 108, 118, 127-132

    Fleet Commands, 139, 141, 144, 148, 149, 157

    Lend-Lease, 19

    Maintenance, 144

  Naval Districts, 115-119

  Procurement and Production, 72, 75-79, 127-130, 132

  Research and Development, 73, 76, 77, 79, 131, 132

Ordnance, Bureau of, 56, 70-79

Ordnance Laboratory, Naval, 131

Ordnance Plants

  Canton, Ohio, 128

  Centerline, Michigan, 128

  Charlotte, North Carolina, 127

  Forest Park, Illinois, 128

  Indianapolis, Indiana, 128

  Pocatello, Idaho, 128

  Shumaker, Arkansas, 127

  South Charleston, West Virginia, 128

  York, Pennsylvania, 128

Ordnance Test Station, Naval, Inyokern, California, 118, 132

Ordway, Samuel H., Jr., Captain, 1

Oregon, 120

Oriental Languages, School of, 125

P

Pacific Beach, California, 152

Pacific, Department of the, U. S. Marine Corps, 46

Pacific Fleet, 149-159

Pacific Fleet and Pacific Ocean Areas, Commander in Chief, United States, 42, 43, 149

Packaging and Materials Handling, 98

Palmyra Atoll, 121

Panamá, 122, 171

Panama Sea Frontier, 122

Parris Island, South Carolina, 113

Pasadena, California, 132

Patents, 73

Patents and Inventions, Office of, 8

Patten, M. T., Lieutenant, App. A

Patuxent River, Maryland, 126, 127

Paymaster, U. S. Marine Corps, 46

Pearl Harbor, Hawaii, 68, 121, 170

Pence, H. L., Captain, 23

Pennsylvania, 91, 111, 128

Pensacola, Florida, 33, 34

Personnel, 4, 48, 53, 80-88, 90, 99, 111, 112, 123, 127, 128, 132, 134, 148, 149, 157, 162; See also Civilians, Black Personnel, Women's Reserve

Assignment, 74, 82, 83, 87, 88, 163, 171, 172

   Aviation, 31, 40, 48, 53, 59, 87

   Classification, 40, 74, 82, 87

   Discipline, 82, 87, 88

   Enlisted, 40, 83, 87, 172

   Officer, 74, 82, 83, 90, 99, 109, 172

   Offices, 81-83, 114, 118, 119, 130, 144, 155, 166

   Planning, 31, 81, 83, 99

   Policy, 80, 81, 109

   Promotion, 74, 82, 87

   Reserve, 40, 99

   Separation, 74, 82, 109

   Training, 59, 74, 81, 83, 87, 88, 99, 109, 172

Personnel, Bureau of Naval, 41, 80-88, 99, 105

Personnel Center, Naval, NOB Terminal Island, California, 169

Personnel Division, Office of the Deputy Chief of Naval Operations (Air), 41

Peters, E. R., Lieutenant Commander, App. A

Petroleum, 13, 24, 94, 155, 164; See also Army-Navy Petroleum Board, Fuel, Tankers

Petroleum-Tanker Division, 13

Pettee, Everette E., Commander, 88

Philadelphia Navy Yard, 111

Philadelphia, Pennsylvania, 91, 111

Philippine Islands Campaign, 42, 68, 159

Philippine Sea Frontier, 159

Photographic Intelligence Center, Naval, 129

Photography, 61, 129, 149, 155

Physical Fitness Programs, 83

Planning, 17, 18, 23, 49, 55, 60, 69, 71, 101, 148

    Aviation, 52, 58, 60, 62

    Commands and Offices, 3, 10, 18, 46, 71, 81, 101, 110, 115, 118, 119, 163

    Logistics, 18, 101

    Operational, 15, 68, 110, 115, 139, 145, 147, 153, 168

    Personnel, 81, 99

    Post-World War II, 73, 157, 162

    Procurement and Production, 3, 22, 52

Planning and Control Activity, Bureau of Naval Personnel, 81

Planning Division, Bureau of Supplies and Accounts, 106

Planning and Progress Division, Bureau of Ordnance, 71

Planning and Statistics Branch, Office of Procurement and Material, 3

Plans and Operations Division, Bureau of Naval Personnel, 81

Plastics, 76

Pocatello, Idaho, 128

Point Molate, California, 133

Port Armstrong, Alaska, 156

Port Chicago, California, 127

Port Directors, Naval

    Eighth Naval District, 115

    Fifteenth Naval District, 122

    Fifth Naval District, 112

    First Naval District, 109

    Naval Transportation Service, 121

    New York, 110

    Ninth Naval District, 116

    Sixth Naval District, 113

    Twelfth Naval District, 119

Port Hueneme, California, 150, 169

Portland, Maine, 109

Port Operations, 157

Ports and Bases, Germany, 147

Portsmouth Naval Shipyard, Portsmouth, New Hampshire, 109

Portsmouth, New Hampshire, 109

Postal Service, 16, 147, 149, 155, 158

Postgraduate School, Severn River Naval Command, 136

Post-World War II, 52, 74, 111, 147, 157, 162

Potomac River Naval Command, 129, 135

Potts, John, Colonel, App. A

Powder Factory, Naval, Indianhead, Maryland, 132

Powel, Robert J. H., 8, 130, App. A

Price Adjustment Board, 7

Princeton University, 23

Procurement, 2, 19, 22, 53, 61, 72, 92, 102, 109, 111, 130

    Aviation, 31, 37-39, 53, 62, 91

    Fuel, 94, 102

    Offices and Units, 2-4, 22, 38, 110

    Ordnance, 75, 76

    Policy, 94, 102, 104

    Raw Materials, 2-4, 22

    Subsistence, 92, 102, 104

Procurement and Material, Office of, 2-6, 38, 98

Procurement Branch, Office of Procurement and Material, 5

Production, 4, 89, 109, 123; See also Industrial Mobilization, Procurement

    Aviation, 38, 52-54

    Ordnance, 15, 75, 77, 79, 127, 129, 130, 132

    Policy, 53, 75

Production Division, Bureau of Ordnance, 72

Program Planning Section, Aviation Planning Division, 31

Programs and Allocations Section, Aviation Planning Division, 31

Progress Section, Office of the Chief of Naval Operations, 17

Projectiles, 76; See also Ordnance

Property Transportation Office, First Naval District, 109

Proving Ground, Naval, Dahlgren, Virginia, 132

Psychological Warfare, 149

PT Boats; See Motor Torpedo Boats

Publications, 63, 70, 81, 101, 123, 124; See also Registered Publications

    Official, 82, 83, 85, 86, 93

Public Information, Office of, Chaplains' Division, Bureau of Naval Personnel, 86

Public Relations and Information, 70, 86, 88, 101, 111, 149

    Activities and Offices, 86, 114, 119, 121, 158, 163, 169

Public Relations Office, First Naval District, 109

Public Works, 108, 111; See also Maintenance, Construction

Puerto Castilla, Honduras, 122

Puerto Rico, 160

Puget Sound Navy Yard, Washington, 152

Purchase Division, Bureau of Supplies and Accounts, 102, 103

Putnam, Hamilton S., Lieutenant, 145, App. A

Pyle, Norman R., 48, 53, 54, 58-60, 64, 66

Pyrotechnics, 77, 78, 131; See also Ordnance

Q

Quality Control Division, Bureau of Naval Personnel, 83

Quartermaster, U. S. Marine Corps, 46

Quincy, Massachusetts, 109

Quonset Point, Rhode Island, 32, 109

R

Radar, 38, 109, 110

Radford Board, 91

Radio Direction Finders, 162

Radio Service, Naval, 16; See also Communications

Radio Stations, Naval

    Farfan, Panama, 122

    Gatun, Panama, 122

    Greenland, 140

    Severn River Naval Command, 136

    Summit, Panama, 122

Raleigh, North Carolina, 113

Receiving Station and Disciplinary Barracks, Naval, NOB Terminal Island, California, 169

Recife, Brazil, 146

Records and Library, Office of Naval, 26; See also History, Office of Naval

Records and Transportation Activity, Bureau of Naval Personnel, 86

Records Division, Bureau of Naval Personnel, 86

Recreation, 85, 121, 144, 149

<u>Recreation Journal</u>, 85

Recruitment, 1, 46, 82, 83, 87-89, 99, 118, 172

Registered Publications, 16; See also Publications

Reinke, William F., 48, 58

Repair; See Shipbuilding and Repair

Research and Development, 8, 9, 65, 83, 89, 92, 170; See also Science

    Aviation, 48, 57, 62, 65

    Commands and Units, 8, 9, 25, 57, 73, 83

    Ordnance, 15, 73, 75-79, 130-132

Research and Development Division, Bureau of Ordnance, 73

Research, Development and Storage Projects Section, Planning Division, Bureau of Supplies and Accounts, 106

Research and Inventions, Office of, 8, 134

Research Laboratory, Naval, 8, 134

Reserve, Naval, 40, 116

<u>Reserve Register</u>, 82

Reykjavik, Iceland, 168

Reynolds, Jack A., Lieutenant, 162, App. A

Rhode Island, 32, 109, 130, 171

Risk, James C., Lieutenant Commander, 148

Rockets and Guided Missiles, 76, 77-79, 128, 132;
    See also Ordnance

Roi-Namur, 157

Roland, Leo J., Lieutenant, 122, App. A

Rouse, Hubert B. Commander, 169

Rowland, Thomas B., Lieutenant, App. A

Rubber, 2, 102

Russell, Christopher A., Commander, 112, App. A

Russia; See Union of Soviet Socialist Republics

Russian Language, 125

S

St. John's, Newfoundland, 139

St. Juliens Creek, Virginia, 127

St. Lucia Island, 166

Salerno Invasion, 68, 148

Salvage, 89, 155

San Diego, California, 33, 118, 152

San Francisco, California, 107, 119, 132, 163

San Juan, Puerto Rico, 117

San Pedro, California, 152, 169

Santa Barbara, California, 118

Sardinia, 108, 148

Savannah, Georgia, 113

Scandinavia, 147

Schools, 83, 88, 108, 109, 125, 129, 141, 145; See also Training, Specific Schools

    Naval Academy, 33, 136, 137

    Technical, 33, 35, 83, 109, 125, 132, 136, 141, 143, 145, 152, 171

Schultz, Harold S., Ensign, App. A

Science, 8, 25, 29, 131, 134, 162; See also Research and Development

Scotland, 139

Seabees; See Construction Battalions

Sea Frontiers, 45, 160-169; See also Individual Sea Frontiers

Seal Beach, California, 118

Seattle, Washington, 120

Secretary of the Navy, Office of, 1-9, 134

Section Base, Naval, San Francisco, California, 119

Security, 49, 70, 132; See also Harbor Defense, Local Defense Units and Activities, 14, 116, 119, 121, 136

Security Office, First Naval District, 109

Selective Service System, 87, 109, 118

Selph, V. P., Lieutenant, 13

Senior Naval Officer Present (Ashore), Baltimore, Maryland, 112

Service Force, U. S. Atlantic Fleet, 144

Service Force, U. S. Pacific Fleet, 155

Service Squadrons Two, Three, Four, Six, Seven, Eight, Nine, Ten, Twelve, Fourteen, 155

Seventeenth Naval District, 46, 156

Seventh Fleet, 15

Seventh Naval District, 114, 159, 162

Severn River Naval Command, 135, 136

Seward, Alaska, 156

Shakedown School, San Diego, California, 152

Shanahan, William O., Lieutenant Commander, 37, 38, App. A

Shannon Island, 140

Shipbuilding and Repair, 14, 20, 87, 93, 120, 145, 155, 163, 165; See also Maintenance, Navy Yards

    Facilities and Units, 14, 89, 108, 109, 111, 112, 120, 129, 136, 169

Ship Characteristics and Fleet Requirements Subsection, Bureau of Ordnance, 73

Shipping (Military), 11, 13, 24, 110, 121, 154; See also Merchant Shipping

Ships and Advanced Base Section, Transportation Division, Bureau of Supplies and Accounts, 107

Ships and Craft; See Individual Ship Types

Ships, Bureau of, 134

Ship's Service Stores, 85, 105, 121

Ship's Store Division, Bureau of Supplies and Accounts, 105

Shipyards (Commercial), 14, 109, 170; See also Navy Yards, Shipbuilding and Repair

Shoemaker, California, 119

Shumaker, Arkansas, 127

Sicily, 68, 138, 148

Siebert, Russell, Lieutenant, 83, App. A

Simons, G. P., Lieutenant Commander, App. A

Sitka, Alaska, 156

Sixth Naval District, 113

Small Craft School, San Pedro, California, 152

Small Craft Training Center, NOB Terminal Island, California, 169

Smith College, 109

Smith, Edna L., Second Lieutenant, App. A

Smith, J. Clovis, Lieutenant Commander, 122

Smith, Mapheus, Dr., 47-58, 61-67

Smith, P. S., Lieutenant, App. A

Solomon Islands Campaign, 68, 154

Solomons, Maryland, 132

Sonar, 138

Sound School, San Diego, California, 152

South America, 146; See also Individual Countries

South Atlantic Force, 138, 146

South Carolina, 113

South Charleston, West Virginia, 128

South Greenland Patrol, 140

Southwest Pacific Area, Commander, 154, 159

Southwest Pacific Sea Frontier, 159

Soviet Union; See Union of Soviet Socialist Republics

Special Assistant and Director of Public Information, Office of the Bureau of Naval Personnel, 86

Special Board on Naval Ordnance, 74

Special Devices Division, Bureau of Aeronautics, 8

Special Services Division, Bureau of Naval Personnel, 85

Spencer, Ivor D., Lieutenant, 32

Spencer, Ralph D., Lieutenant (junior grade), 157

Sprinz, P. T., Lieutenant, App. A

Standards and Curriculum Division, Bureau of Naval Personnel, 83

Standards Division, Bureau of Supplies and Accounts, 96

Standard Stock Catalog, Navy, 95

Stanwood, Charles F., Lieutenant, 30, App. A

Stations, Naval

    Guantanamo, Cuba, 165

    Toboga, Panama, 171

Statistics, 3, 59, 70-72, 123

Steel, 4

Stevenson, Hollice E., Lieutenant, 157, App. A

Stillwater, Oklahoma, 88

Stock Division, Bureau of Supplies and Accounts, 95, 106

Stockley, Louise T., Lieutenant (junior grade), 88, App. A

Stockton, Bee, 48-50, 67

Stockton, California, 133

Storage, 94, 106, 127, 133, 164, 168

Storage Division, Bureau of Supplies and Accounts, 106

Storage Section, Stock Division, Bureau of Supplies and Accounts, 106

Strayer, Paul J., Lieutenant, App. A

Stuit, Dewey B., Lieutenant Commander, 83

Submarine Forces

    Atlantic Fleet, 170

    Pacific Fleet, 170

Submarines, 20, 32, 78, 159, 170; See also Antisubmarine Warfare

    Enemy, 11, 112, 140-142, 146, 160, 162, 167

Submarines Atlantic Fleet, 170

Submarines Southwest Pacific, 170

Subsistence and Clothing Division, Bureau of Supplies and Accounts, 92

Subsistence Division, Bureau of Supplies and Accounts, 104

Summit, Panama, 122

Supervisor of Shipbuilding, Newport News, Virginia, 112

Supervisor of Shipbuilding, Severn River Naval Command, 136

Supplies and Accounts, Bureau of, 90-107

Supply, 56, 100, 101, 144, 163; See also Materials

    Facilities and Units, 106, 108, 116, 119, 133

    Ordnance Materials, 71, 73

Supply Corps, 99, 102

Supply Depot, Naval, Oakland, California, 133

Supply Sub-depot, Navy, Stockton, California, 133

Support Force, Atlantic Fleet, 139, 140

Supreme Headquarters, Allied Expeditionary Force, 25

Surabaya, Java, 170

Surinam, 166

T

Taboga Island, Panama, 122, 171

Taboguilla Island, 122

Talbot, Melvin F., Commander, 148

Talmage, John R., Lieutenant, 96, 97

Tankers, 13, 24, 164; See also Merchant Shipping, Convoys, Petroleum

Target Repair Base, NOB Terminal Island, California, 169

Task Forces

    Three, 146

    Twenty-Three, 146

    Twenty-Four, 139

    Twenty-Seven, 146

    Ninety-Six, 157

    One Hundred Twenty-Four, 147

    One Hundred Twenty-Six, 147

Task Group 02.4 (Delaware Group), Eastern Sea Frontier, 111

Technical Mission in Europe, Naval, 25

Technical Services Corporation, 47

Technology; See Research and Development

Tele-Typewriter System, Naval (NTX), 16

Tenth Fleet, 10, 11

Tenth Naval District, 117, 160

Terminal Island, California, 169

Test and Research Section, Bureau of Naval Personnel, 83

Third Naval District, 109, 110, 161

Thirteenth Naval District, 120, 156, 163

Thoma, Henry, Lieutenant, 83

Thomas, W. S., Lieutenant, App. A

Thompson, Howard J., Lieutenant (junior grade), 151

Thompson, Laurance R., Lieutenant Commander, App. A

Thompson, Robert L., Lieutenant (junior grade), App. A

Tiburon, California, 132

Time Service, U. S. Naval Observatory, 124

Tobias, George, Lieutenant, 38

Torpedos, 51, 76, 78, 109, 128, 130, 151; See also Ordnance

Torpedo Station, Naval, Newport, Rhode Island, 109, 130

Traffic Section, Fuel and Transportation Division, Bureau of Supplies and Accounts, 107

Train Squadron Six, 153

Training, 1, 8, 33-35, 46, 48, 59, 61, 74, 84, 87, 111, 134, 141, 144, 154, 167, 170; See also Schools

    Aviation, 29, 33-36, 41, 48, 59, 61, 67

    Commands and Offices, 41, 81, 83, 109, 121, 122, 143, 145, 150, 152, 157, 165, 166, 169

    Enlisted, 171, 172

    Medical, 68, 69

    Officer, 23, 99, 137, 171, 172

    Reserve, 88, 137

    Technical, 78, 83, 109, 110, 118, 125, 128, 129, 131, 132, 150, 151

Training Activity, Bureau of Naval Personnel, 83

Training Aids Division, Bureau of Naval Personnel, 83

Training and Distribution Centers, Naval

    Camp Peary, Virginia, 112

    Treasure Island, California, 119

Training Centers, Naval

    Bainbridge, Maryland, 112

    Great Lakes, Illinois, 83

Training Command, Amphibious Forces, 150

Training Schools, Naval

    Bronx, New York, 88

    Cedar Falls, Iowa, 88

    Stillwater, Oklahoma, 88

Training Station, Naval, NOB Norfolk, Virginia, 112

Transportation, 86, 94, 97, 98, 104, 107, 112, 133, 169; See also Merchant Shipping, Supply

    Air, 29, 50, 107, 157, 158, 163

    Facilities, 77, 107

    Offices and Units, 17, 24, 86, 107, 116, 118, 119, 121, 144, 157

    Personnel, 86, 97

Transportation Division, Bureau of Naval Personnel, 86

Transportation Division, Bureau of Supplies and Accounts, 107

Transportation Section, Naval, Office of the Chief of Naval Operations, 17

Transportation Service, Naval, 24, 29, 121

Treasure Island, California, 119

Tredinnick, Frank A., Jr., 171

Trinidad, 108, 160, 166

Trinidad Sector, Caribbean Sea Frontier, 166

Turnbull, Archibald D., 28

Twelfth Naval District, 46, 119, 163

U

U-Boats; See Submarines

Under Secretary of the Navy, Office of, 7

Underwater Demolition Teams, Commander, 150

Uniforms, 65, 82, 92; See also Clothing

Union of Soviet Socialist Republics, 120

United Kingdom; See Great Britain

United States Fleet, Commander in Chief, 10-12, 45

Universities; See Individual Schools

University of California at Berkeley, 125

University of Colorado, 125

Uruguay, 146

Utah, 119

U. S.-Allied Relations, 94, 146, 167
    Lend-Lease, 19, 38, 64, 97

V

V-12 Program, 83

Van der Poel, P. G., Lieutenant Commander, App. A

Van Wyen, Adrian O., Lieutenant, 43, 44, App. A

Vaupel, Ann Fortune, First Lieutenant, 34, App. A

Venereal Disease, 109

Virginia, 33, 112, 127, 132, 135, 142, 144

Voge, Richard G., Captain, 170

W

Wales, Kenneth S., Lieutenant Commander, 166

Walker, L. Rohn, Lieutenant Commander, 4

War Bonds, 109, 115

War Manpower Commission, 83

War Plans; See Planning

War Production Board, 2-4

War Shipping Administration, 24

Wartime Merchant Ship Communications School, NOB Terminal Island, California, 169

Washington (State), 120, 152

Washington Atoll, 121

Washington Navy Yard, 129, 135

Waves; See Women's Reserve

Weapons; See Ordnance

Weather Central, Navy, 122

Weems, Robert C., Lieutenant Commander, 41

Welfare Activity, Bureau of Naval Personnel, 85

Wendell, W. G., Captain, App. A

Western Sea Frontier, 118, 163

West Virginia, 112, 128

White, H. Lee, Commander, 1

Whitehill, Walter Muir, Commander, 10, App. A

Wildwood, New Jersey, 111

Williams, Robert P., Lieutenant (junior grade), 96

Williamsburg, Virginia, 112

Willow Grove, Pennsylvania, 111

Woodbury, Robert, Commander, App. A

Women's Reserve, 46, 88, 118, 135

    Naval District Administration, 109, 113, 115, 116, 119

Women's Reserve School, Smith College, Northampton, Massachusetts, 109

World War I, 22, 112, 116

    Aviation, 28, 32, 33, 37, 40

Wright, George H., Lieutenant (junior grade), App. A

Wyoming, 120

Y

Yale University, 28

Yards and Docks, Bureau of, 14, 58, 108

Yarnell, H. E., Admiral, 27, 91

Yarnell Report, 91

Yerba Buena Island, San Francisco, California, 119

York, Pennsylvania, 128

Yorktown, Virginia, 132

Z

Zubrow, Solomon E., Lieutenant Commander, 111

www.ingramcontent.com/pod-product-compliance
Lightning Source LLC
Chambersburg PA
CBHW081833170426
43199CB00017B/2718